What Others are Saying about
MY HOUSE OUR HOUSE

"The story of how Karen, Louise and Jean created a successful shared home should encourage everyone who has playfully or seriously said, 'When we retire, let's live together.' Read it, and you may find yourself saying, 'Why not now?'"

– Annamarie Pluhar, author of
Sharing Housing: A Guidebook for Finding and Keeping Good Housemates

"This wonderful book is a MUST for mature adults interested in responsibly facing the third phase of their lives."

– Oz Ragland, retired Executive Director of the Cohousing Association, and Instigator of the Cohouseholding Project

"I am so pleased to see a book that gives practical, real-life examples, information, and encouragement for women who wish to live together in a cooperative household. Thank you, Karen, Louise and Jean, for writing this fine book!"

– Joan Medlicott, author of *The Ladies of Covington* novels

"Important practical advice for anyone considering a shared living arrangement. Readers are invited to explore the balance between private and public space, personal and social time, independence and interdependence, individual financial well being and shared costs."

– Maria Piantanida, Ph.D., member, Borland Green intentional community, Pittsburgh, PA

"Bright, witty, deeply sane – this is a wonderful book. I defy anyone who starts reading it to put it down. Even the legal stuff is eminently readable, and that is no small praise. I would be proud to call these marvelous ladies my friends."

– Liz Gilbey, journalist, United Kingdom

"Men, listen up: Keep this book away from your wives. If they find out how much fun it can be to share a home with their friends, we're history. These three women bought a nicer house than any of them could afford separately and they annoy each other by being too helpful. I fear it's over for us, boys."

– Brian O'Neill, Pittsburgh Post-Gazette columnist, author of *The Paris of Appalachia: Pittsburgh in the Twenty-First Century*

"My House Our House combines the best of all worlds in one easy-to-read book for those wanting an alternative housing choice."

– Marianne Kilkenny, Founder and Grand Nudge, Women for Living in Community

"A must-read for anyone considering cooperative housing. It could well become the Strunk and White of the shared living movement. The book transcends being a mere 'how to'."

– John Armstrong, business writer and retired Manager of Public Affairs, U.S. Steel Corp.

"My House Our House *thinks outside the box on living options. An engaging, enlightening and inspiring read. I highly recommend this book.*"

– Nancy Chubb, Ph.D., M.B.A., psychologist and life coach

"I love this book! It is loaded with practical ideas and insights about how to make cooperative living work."

– Maureen Murray, national speaker, trainer and coach

"Together, these three feisty, courageous women have created a unique living arrangement that capitalizes on strengths, compensates for weaknesses, furnishes a greatly enhanced quality of life – and serves as a true inspiration for us all! "

– Rita Levine, reporter/writer, *mt. lebanon magazine*

My House
Our House

MY HOUSE OUR HOUSE

Living Far Better for Far Less
in a Cooperative Household

KAREN M.
BUSH

LOUISE S.
MACHINIST

JEAN
McQUILLIN

st. lynn's
press

PITTSBURGH

My House Our House
Living Far Better for Far Less in a Cooperative Household

ISBN-13: 978-0-9855622-4-3

Library of Congress Control Number: 2013936267
CIP information available upon request

First Edition, 2013

St. Lynn's Press • POB 18680 • Pittsburgh, PA 15236
412.466.0790 • www.stlynnspress.com

Book design–Holly Rosborough
Editor–Catherine Dees
Editorial Intern–Marguerite Nocchi

Photo credits:
Front and back covers, pages xiv, 31, 40, 48, 163, 192 – Holly Rosborough
All other photos by MHOH friends and family

Printed in The United States of America
On certified FSC recycled paper using soy-based inks

This title and all of St. Lynn's Press books may be purchased for educational, business, or sales promotional use. For information please write:
Special Markets Department . St. Lynn's Press .
POB 18680 . Pittsburgh, PA 15236

10 9 8 7 6 5 4 3 2 1

If I am who I am because I am who I am and you are who you are because you are who you are then I am who I am and you are who you are, but if I am who I am because you are who you are and you are who you are because I am who I am then I am not who I am and you are not who you are.

YASMINA REZA, FROM *ART*

Table of Contents

Jean	Karen	Louise
11	9	6

Foreword

Ahh, the longevity revolution! Never have there been so many old people in such good shape in any previous generation. When they say "60 is the new 40" (or some variation of this ridiculous phrase), it means the course of our lives is remaining in play longer. It's a whole new game now, and we're having to make up the rules as we go along. The good news is, we have more years to try new things, prepare our legacy, enrich our experiences – and cultivate relationships that make us wealthy beyond measure.

But as we look forward to this promising phase of life, we start asking ourselves, Where will we live? How will we live? Most of us know we don't want assisted living or independent living or any of the other categories of "senior housing" we know from caring for our parents. We can't picture ourselves subject to the management, the rules, the institutional-ness. We can't picture ourselves in the lobby of those places listening to the Stones on our iPhone. Yet we can't avoid the questions of where and how, as our needs change – because change they will.

I've spent the last twenty years working at better options, designing ways for people to stay in their own homes longer, if they wish, by making simple structural and other adaptations. It's part of a concept called Aging in Place. My career has focused on making our homes the right places to grow old with dignity. One thing I have learned is that aging with dignity is more complex than just space design. Not only is every house different, but every household, every family, every neighborhood and community is different too. Every factor has an impact on one's quality of life. And not all of us want to – or can afford to – stay in our home for the long run.

People who know of my work often tell me their "later-in-life daydreams," that ideal living arrangement that's out there somewhere. Many describe a compound with their own space but the proximity of friends. On the other hand, they don't want it to be like a group house in college, with little privacy or boundaries. It always comes down to, How can I have my privacy without having to live alone?

The three authors of *My House Our House* had their own daydreams as well. And they took action. With intelligence, open minds and a sense of adventure, these members of the Boomer generation crafted an alternative living arrangement they call cooperative householding. And now, many years into their successful experiment, they're here to give us the benefit of their experience. Something like this concept may have been in the back of your mind a few times...or almost the subject of a conversation with some friends. This book moves past your daydreams and past the hard part of exercising your imagination, to offer concrete steps for going forward.

My House Our House is a map to a newly opened frontier.

Some say Boomers like to break the rules, but Karen, Louise and Jean teach us to make new rules – good, thoughtful rules, tested by people you can respect. Don't be snowed by the warm context and fun spirit; this book covers sophisticated and radical ideas. The mark of good communicating is making the complex and important clear and seemingly simple. They write eloquently and thoroughly about details that would not occur to me. They cover tough issues I might avoid. Their book is a template for a good process. They deal with finding and purchasing a house, finding partners, setting up finances, combining furnishings and household routines…and most importantly: how you can know if cooperative householding is for you.

Beyond bringing the logistics of everyday living to daylight in this new and multi-faceted relationship, *My House Our House* is a self-aware discussion for all kinds of relationships – business, family, friends – with value beyond its stated purpose. If you follow these guiding ideas you will be rewarded no matter where you move, with whom you live or even with whom you work.

We Boomers changed every institution we touched throughout our lives. It is not just the size of our cohort; we redefined relationships, families, work. Life. We all want to be independent. Independence means choices and control. But, as we're now discovering, it doesn't require living alone.

And that's what makes Karen, Louise and Jean's story great.

I know the longevity revolution means that change is inevitable. That can be unsettling. We live longer, so our homes must adapt and change. The very concept of households will change as well. Cooperative householding may be a welcome island in the chaos. This book charts the course there. If you have had daydreams – or nightmares – about where you will live in the next stage of your life, read this book. Let it guide you forward into a new and thought-provoking world of possibilities.

Louis Tenenbaum
Aging in Place strategist and consultant, founder of
The Aging In Place Institute, author of *Aging in Place 2.0*.
www.louistenenbaum.com

Welcome!

Prologue

From you I receive,
To you I give.
Together we share,
*And from this we live.**

Nathan Segal, "From You I Receive"

This book tells the story of how three independent women and one very independent black and white cat came to share a home.

In 2004, we three fifty-something Baby Boomers were happily living alone, occasionally pondering what seemed at the time the far-fetched notion of sharing a home together in the distant future, when we retired. Then, the situation changed. Suddenly, almost impulsively, with a scant month of rapid-fire planning, we found ourselves buying a house and preparing to move in together to create a cooperative household.

Startled friends and family members made varying predictions about how long we'd survive our communal living arrangement – none very encouraging. Now, as we find ourselves happily approaching a second decade together, those pre-

---

A framed version of these words hangs in our breakfast room; we sometimes recite them before holiday meals with family and friends.

dictions have been proved wrong. Not only have we survived, we've thrived. And along the way, we've developed a number of tools and resources that we hope will be helpful to anyone thinking about doing what we have done.

We offer this how-to book to get you thinking about a simple-but-effective housing alternative for independent people. Our model of cooperative householding can be created anywhere, at any age or life stage, at any level of housing cost or financial investment. Your lifestyle priorities may not be the same as ours, but we offer examples from our own experience to paint a clear picture of daily life in our community. However, it's not the details of our lifestyle that matter, but the big-picture concepts and how they might apply to your own circumstances.

Please make yourself comfortable while we share our story and encourage you to consider this atypical yet eminently sensible, practical, economical and enjoyable housing option.

We'll begin on the Saturday of Labor Day weekend 2004, the day we hosted a mega open house after living in our new home for just one month. During that marathon event, each of us was asked to tell our story again and again as we guided almost 200 guests through the house from noon until long after midnight. Our friends' and new neighbors' enthusiasm and curiosity carried us well past the point of exhaustion.

Imagine a balmy September evening. You and other guests are just arriving.

ONE

Open House at Shadowlawn

Welcome! We're so glad you could join us for our open house. By the end of the evening, you'll know exactly how three independent adults share communal space, yet create personal space, in ways that make this cooperative household work. But be careful – you might want to move in.

During the house tour, we'll explain how we created the home we fondly call Shadowlawn, derived from the name of our street. We quickly found it useful to have a name for the house, not to be cute, but for ease of communication. After all, this place is "my house," "our house," "your house," "her house," "Jean's house," "Karen's house" and "Louise's house."

Shadowlawn has more dignity than "The Old Biddies' Commune," the humorous name we coined when we first started dreaming about a shared venture. Friends memorialized the acronym by carving "O.B.C." into a large rock, now nestled on the front stoop. They deposited it there in the dark of moving-in night to inaugurate our "commune." It was waiting to surprise us when we opened the door on our first morning in the house. We

Big news! We decided that maintaining three residences didn't make a lot of sense. So we sold our separate houses and bought this lovely home in Mt. Lebanon. Each of us has a separate living area and we share common space and community. Our special place is "Shadowlawn," named after the street adjacent to our backyard.

Jean McQuillin, Karen Bush, & Louise Machinist

Join us at our Open House!
Saturday, September 4, noon to midnight.

We'll supply shish kabob, beverages, and plenty of house tours.
Please bring other foods to share.
(No gifts allowed! Your presence is our present.)

Our Open House Invitation

re-interpret the initials in various ways. We like "Only Beautiful Chicks" best.

Before you come inside, join the group in the backyard. Good thing it's not raining; no way all the guests could fit into the house. We're glad we took the time to ring the yard with tiki torches, creating a shimmering glow on the foliage. The trees and gardens are among the things that made us fall in love with this old house, but none of us could have taken on this kind of lawn maintenance alone.

Exhausted as we are from our move, we're loving the moment. Maybe it was crazy to host a twelve-hour open house and grill dinner for 200 a bare month after moving in, but the adrenaline-fueled adventure of the move has left us feeling like we can tackle anything. Our new-old house looks surprisingly good, certainly the best we could manage in four frantic weeks of coordinating, culling and moving our individual possessions.

The living room may be colonial at one end and contemporary at the other, but the colors blend and the green sofa makes the transition between the wildly different area rug patterns. Everyone's furniture received a place of honor, even though the styles are so different. Jean's softer color palette works well in the little room with the bay window and great view of the backyard and gardens. While we think we've created wonderful harmony out of dissonance, Jean's daughter, Maureen, had a different view of the decor: "Nothing matches, does it?"

Since we moved in, we've felt a bit like trailblazers. On first meeting, people in our new neighborhood frequently exclaim, *Oh! You're one of the three...just like The Golden Girls...How's it going? What you're doing is fascinating...Can I join the "commune"?*

During our first week, Jean went to the bank to change the address on her checking account, and even the teller knew our story. As you can imagine, our neighbors wondered what's up with the three women who just moved in. Many of them are at the open house tonight, and already seem to be getting into the spirit of our adventure.

Please don't be shy. Help yourself to shish kabob – chicken, beef, or tofu – from the grill, drinks from the patio table. We know you won't mind the mismatched assortment of paper plates, napkins and cups at this party. Go ahead: combine the shamrock plate, the Thanksgiving napkin and the Happy Birthday paper cup as you assemble your meal.

The bizarre assortment actually has meaning; it symbolizes in a small way who we are and what we are creating. Those paper plates and napkins are the remnant paper goods from the combined 123 years of our individual adult homemaking. During the house tour, you might be as surprised as we are at how well the eclectic combination of household furnishings works together, considering that all the items were acquired separately during our cumulative 82 years of marriage and 41 years of single living.

Although things appear to be well organized now, we've just barely pulled it together after months of turmoil. Buying this old house on almost a moment's notice turned our lives upside down. We were actually shocked at the sudden way it happened, and so was everyone we knew.

When asked what she thought about our plan to create a cooperative household, one relative returned a terse one-word e-mail: *No*. But once the surprise wore off, we got positive reactions from family, friends and neighbors.

Joining in the communal spirit of the place, some of our guests have been hanging out at the party for many hours. One neighbor realized that her daughter's favorite high school teacher is a guest, a discovery that started a flow of neighborhood teenagers stopping by to meet everyone. Feel free to stay as long as you like.

Be sure to check with George, the tall guy, before you leave. He is so intrigued by this way of living that he started a sign-up sheet for openings at Shadowlawn. Of course, his name is at the top of the list. That would be okay except for two things. First, his wife, Patty, didn't get to the list fast enough and is number six. Second, none of us has any intention of leaving.

In the course of the evening, many people suggested, *You should write a book.* And so we have. But before we get further into our personal story, let's pause for some context.

Surprise! A gift sneaked onto our doorstep in the dark of night...

TWO

Living Alone/Living Together

The company, the conversation, the sharing,
the communication, the knowledge that someone is there.
It must be psychological, because life seems easier
if you have someone going through it with you.

ERIC KLINENBERG, FROM *GOING SOLO*

At the time we launched our "Golden Girls" household, we didn't know anyone who had a similar arrangement in real life, only on TV. For that matter, we knew absolutely nothing about the intentional community movement and very little about the smorgasbord of shared living models that already existed in 2004 and have been skyrocketing in number since then. National and international, big and small, established and experimental, thriving or failing – they reflect visionary efforts to create meaningful community in diverse forms. In the universe of shared living/shared community, cooperative householding is a tiny niche.

We think it's odd that we didn't know about the spectrum of shared living alternatives until we created one ourselves. Oz

Ragland, the Seattle-based Cohousing Project researcher and intentional community veteran, chalked it up to geography: "Well, of course – you live in Pittsburgh. People in progressive hotbeds all over the country have been exploring alternative living options forever."

Now, even Pittsburgh is starting to show its progressive colors, with three cohousing communities in varying stages of existence. It appears we aren't "making it up as we go along" in isolation anymore. We've become part of an emerging network of people who are helping to further define and promote cooperative householding (a.k.a. cohouseholding), as well as other viable and valuable ways to live in community. See, for example, *The Cohouseholding Project,* www.cohouseholding.com.

But we knew none of this when we began our journey.

The Numbers Tell the Story

After the dust of our move settled, we started researching contemporary housing and shared living trends in the United States, and we discovered what we suburbanites somehow hadn't noticed: demographic housing trends in the United States are changing significantly. For the current statistics and in-depth analysis, we went to *Going Solo: The Extraordinary Rise and Surprising Appeal of Living Alone* by Eric Klinenberg (2012), and to the 2010 U. S. Census.

Demographic trends show changing patterns of household composition. The percentage of married couples is shrinking. As of 2010, childless couples and singletons (single people living alone) comprised 56% of American households. Baby Boomers are in transition and living longer. Multiple causal factors associated with changes in household composition include new employment/work patterns, cultural shifts (most women are employed and financially independent, for one) and the impact of rising energy and transportation costs on housing choices.

The 2008 bursting housing bubble and the economic recession altered the incomes, lifestyle options and priorities of many Americans. Nonetheless, single-person households continue to be on the rise – 28% nationally, 41% in our nearby city and 33% in our own traditional "family community" – despite the financial crunch.

Living Alone: Single Families/Single People

Single heads of households cover the age spectrum: younger singles (including single parents of dependent children) on one end, senior citizens on the other. Klinenberg interviewed many adults living solo who are happy, even delighted, with their lifestyle choice. However, his book provides a balanced picture of the cons as well as the pros, the ambivalence and the tradeoffs. For singletons of any age, living alone can be stressful. For example, many young singles contend with the competing demands of jobs, children, home maintenance and myriad other responsibilities with little or no extended family or community support. At the other end of the spectrum, 79% of Americans age 65 and older still own their own homes, maintaining them with various degrees of success and satisfaction, and facing the possibility of increasing isolation over their senior years. Loneliness can and does affect people of any age.

But There Are So Many Good Options!

The idea of communal housing is not new, but it remains a rare lifestyle choice for Americans. While many people choose to live alone, others don't prefer single living, but believe that circumstances simply leave them no other option. Some people imagine innovative options, yet perceive a huge step from imagining a non-traditional living arrangement to taking the leap. Here's how we know that. In our workshops on cooperative householding, we've met a surprising number of women who have considered the idea of living with sisters, cousins, college roommates, best friends, or joining with their partner and other couples; you name it. Their eyes light up when they hear our story – but then they tell us they haven't done it because they just couldn't visualize how to turn the dream into reality. At least "not yet."

Actually, the innovative Baby Boomer generation is busily exploring alternative ways to address the downsides of single living. They are seeking and finding novel solutions to many practical, economic, social and safety issues, innovations made possible by freer attitudes about lifestyle choices and an expanded sense of community.

To some extent, necessity is the mother of invention. As fewer individuals remain "coupled" for life and incomes or other resources are stretched thin, new ways to manage emerge. In a mobile society, support systems are often based on proximity to friends and acquaintances rather than to biological families; it is increasingly difficult to maintain multi-generational nuclear or extended family households, although there is a growing trend for adult children and their parents to cohabitate.

Let's take a quick look at some non-traditional group living situations that fall under the big umbrellas of intentional community and shared housing.

Living Together: Intentional and Shared Housing Alternatives

"Intentional community" is best defined by the people who live it. Diane Leafe Christian, a longtime member of intentional communities and recognized author on the topic, describes intentional community this way: *"A group of people who have chosen to live together with a common purpose, working cooperatively to create a lifestyle that reflects their shared core values."* Those core values typically include idealism and equality (D.L. Christian, the Fellowship for Intentional Community Directory).

And from the Meadowdance.org website:

> *In essence, an intentional community is a group of people coming together in a place they create to live in some particular way. The variety of intentional communities is nearly infinite: some are religious, some are not; politics run the gamut; they are large and small, rural and urban, ecologically minded and materialistic. They include monasteries, communes, anarchic squatter houses, cooperative housing, co-housing, kibbutzim, Christian activist communities, Shaker communities, and many other kinds of groups.*

Awareness of non-traditional shared living situations has increased exponentially from the 1980s, when people began to write about their experiences and to create community websites.

One of the innovators was gerontologist Jane Porcino, Ph.D., who studied alternative housing options for older women. She noted that the number-one stressor for women at or beyond midlife is a major change in living circumstances (death of spouse, divorce, financial or health problems). And yet, she found that few people proactively design the living arrangement that best meets their needs. She and her husband joined several other couples to develop integrated, yet separate, households in an urban cooperative apartment complex. Their small community offered privacy for each couple as well as mutual support.

To help people start thinking of positive options, her 1991 book, *Living Longer, Living Better: Adventures in Community*

Housing for Those in the Second Half of Life, described four-teen types of alternative communities, ranging from "accessory apartments" through the alphabet to "retirement communities." In the intervening years, an even more varied set of options has emerged. Here are some brief sketches of several of those models:

- **Cohousing Communities** Architects Charles Durrett and Kathryn McCamant are the pioneers of the American cohousing movement. They studied well-established cohousing villages in Denmark and other European countries and brought the model here. Cohousing communities are carefully planned villages that combine individual houses with shared facilities for people of all ages. Residents design and manage the community, generally through consensus governance. They volunteer for community tasks, like maintenance and preparing shared meals.

   The daunting planning phase of a new cohousing development typically takes several arduous years, from inception to investment, site selection, construction, and creating community. (See pages 184-185 for cohousing publications by Durrett, McCamant and others.)

   In the years since the first U.S. cohousing community opened in 1991, cohousing has burgeoned. The 2011 *Cohousing Association of the United States Directory* lists 233 sites. But cohousing has not yet come to all parts of the country, and other forms of intentional community are emerging as well.

- **The Fellowship for Intentional Community** To start with, here is the go-to site for a broad overview and lots of information: http://fic.ic.org/. Established in its current form in 1986, the Fellowship for Intentional Community

(FIC) publishes a hugely informative, multifaceted website and a community directory. At one glance, you will grasp the great diversity of non-traditional community living options in the United States. The 2012 FIC *Communities Directory* lists 1,055 entries, and those are just the communities that self-submit a listing (only non-coercive/nonviolent community listings are accepted.) The FIC mission is to *"nurture connections and cooperation among communitarians and their friends"* and to foster public awareness. The idealism of the Fellowship is reflected in their self-description: *"a small group of dedicated individuals trying to change the world."* By their latest estimate, 100,000 Americans currently live in an intentional community of some type, including ecovillages and other environmental and social justice-oriented groups (see Geoph Kozeny, "In Community Intentionally," FIC *Communities Directory*, pgs. 7 and 14). One subset of these, the Federation of Egalitarian Communities, is *"a union of egalitarian communities which have joined together in our common struggle to create a lifestyle based on equality, cooperation, and harmony with the earth."* Different from most cohousing communities, the FEC communities generate and share income as a group.

• **Home-Sharing, a.k.a. Homesharing** Local and national media periodically spotlight stories of contemporary "Golden Girls," small groups of women who share a home. These stories are reminiscent of the *Ladies of Covington* novels by Joan Medlicott, hopefully with less emotional drama for the inhabitants. Interestingly, we haven't stumbled upon similar news features about independent single men living in shared housing groups, but they must exist.

Also called a "share house," the "housemates" or "roommates" most often share a rented residence, but many variations are possible, including owner-occupiers renting space to the others. Residents are typically not related and not expecting a long-term arrangement. Annamarie Pluhar's book, *Sharing Housing,* offers comprehensive guidelines about finding appropriate roommates and avoiding potential pitfalls.

There are social service agencies that organize home-sharing for individuals with special needs, financial or physical. The aim is to match individuals compatibly, for mutual benefit.

- **Pocket Neighborhoods** Architect Ross Chapin designs small neighborhoods of eight to ten clustered houses around a shared landscaped commons. The homeowners can readily get to know each other and interact in a more bonded way than in typical single-family housing developments. This ready-made neighborhood avoids the time and resource-consuming organizational process – and the more intensive level of mutual commitment – of a cohousing community. (See Ross Chapin's *Pocket Neighborhoods* (2011) and http://pocket-neighborhoods.net/index.html)

- **Retirement Communities** Retirement Communities (not covered here) include, but are not limited to, facilities that offer a spectrum of options, from fully independent living through assisted living and nursing care.

- **Aging in Place/Aging in Community** The groundbreaking work of Ken Dychtwald, Louis Tenenbaum and other visionaries has been a catalyst to re-imagining lifestyle options for seniors.

Though not a specific type of living arrangement, the Aging in Place (AIP) movement promotes state-of-the-art home design, assistive technology and multi-service integration, to enable people to remain in the homes they want to live in, with maximum independence and safety, for as long as possible. AIP may or may not include shared housing in one form or another. For more about Aging in Place, see www.louistenenbaum.com.

The Aging in Community movement is inventing innovative models of senior cohousing, shared housing, and associated "village" networks. References include Raines Cohen, www.agingincommunity.com, and *Audacious Aging: Eldership As a Revolutionary Endeavor,* edited by Stephanie Marohn.

Our Model: Living Independently, Together, Through Cooperative Householding

The stories of people who have dedicated their time, money, lives and livelihoods to the utopian dream of building better ways to live in community are truly inspiring. In Paul Ray's wonderful phrase, these are true "cultural creatives." (See David Wann, "Reinventing Community," FIC *Directory,* pg. 7.) In contrast, we followed a much more pragmatic path than an idealistic one. We were motivated primarily by the immediate practical benefits to each of us, and were secondarily aware of the less tangible but broader ramifications for environmental, social and cultural change.

Unlike larger intentional communities, we did not spend years in careful discernment about a shared vision or to establish complex community governance and covenants; we did not need to acquire significant capital or embark on a major construction project. But there are similarities between our model of shared living and others: we proactively found ways to solve problems of living in atypical ways. In certain respects, we probably re-invented the wheel, instead of learning from what other shared housing folks were already doing. Since you are reading this book, at least you won't have to start from scratch.

We call our shared living model cooperative householding, using the "ing" gerund form to emphasize that this is an active, evolving process, not just a place.

Here's how we define our model of shared living:

> **Cooperative householding:** *A shared housing partnership of two or more unrelated people who co-own, reside in, and jointly manage a residence to gain financial, social, lifestyle, environmental and/or other benefits.* (By "unrelated," we mean that the housemates are homeowner partners, not a nuclear family or a romantic partnership.)

Of course, cooperative householding shares elements with other types of group living, in particular, shared housing/home sharing. What is different is the co-ownership of the residence, an ingredient that we believe is essential from psychological and legal standpoints to ensure equality, i.e., equal power, equal commitment, and equal responsibility, among the partners. Here are the important expectations that come with and derive from our cooperative householding model:

1. Co-owned, co-equal and co-operative.
2. Long-term commitment, but not assumed to be permanent.
3. The partners are independent, not dependent on each other, despite interdependent homeownership.

As co-homeowners, we hold equal shares in each and every aspect of homeownership.

In our cooperative household, we devised our own way to live economically, reaping rich advantages: savings in money, time, labor and environmental impact. In our own way, we created a small community that is also rich in mutual support and fun. From a practical standpoint, we enhanced each member's lifestyle, at the same time protecting privacy and independence.

Does this sound far-fetched and unrealistic? That's how it struck Jean's niece, Goldyn – but not for long.

Honestly? Although outwardly supportive, I thought my aunt was crazy: she and two friends buying a house together?! The first thing that came to my mind was MID-LIFE CRISIS. When I think back to why I thought it so strange, I can't come up with a good answer, other than I had never heard of anyone else doing it.

Today, I think it's a marvelous idea and really awesome living arrangement. I have no idea why more people don't do it! Living with good friends while having a separate living space and not having to share a bathroom is really ingenious.

When I go to my aunt's house, it doesn't feel like I am visiting one aunt but more like visiting three. They all know the details of my life, and when we see each other after a long time, we pick right back up where we left off.

It's guaranteed that each evening will end with a glass of wine next to the fire (I usually visit in winter) and excellent conversation, gossip, or both. It's just like coming home.

As an outsider looking into Shadowlawn, it's nice to see that they have each other to share not only the day-to-day experiences but also the peaks and valleys of life. It's a built-in support system in many ways; like any other family but with less drama. I will react differently the next time someone tells me they're going to enter a similar living arrangement.

Think about it: if you live alone and have a free evening, how do you spend it? Watching TV by yourself, like many Americans? In our house, one of the three of us will typically suggest a walk, a game *(Scrabble, anybody?)*, a movie, initiate engaging conversation or just plain relaxation. In inviting weather, we take a cold drink out to the "grotto" (a small area under tall trees at the very back of our garden) to get away from it all within just a few feet of our back door.

These little daily social interactions make for a much healthier and happier style of living than the silence of living alone. Yet each of us can and does opt out when we prefer not to join the others. We all need and respect the beauty of solitude as well as socialization. We have the best of both worlds. And we can answer the thought question posed by *Women for Living in Community* trailblazer Marianne Kilkenny: *Who will leave the lights on for you?*

To learn more about the many possible ways to live together and to share resources, we invite you to explore our resource list at the end of the book. We find a number of sources to be particularly helpful, including: *Creating Community Anywhere* (C.R. Shaffer), *The Sharing Solution* (Janelle Orsi and Emily Doskow), *Sharing Housing* (Annamarie Pluhar), and Marianne Kilkenny's *Women for Living in Community* website, (www.womenlivingincommunity.com).

The chapters that follow offer insider tips about how to create a successful cooperative household. Come with us, retrospectively, on our adventure.

THREE

True Colors:

Meet the Cooperative Householders

First, we'd like you to know a little about each of us, in her own words – about our professions, our families, what is important to us individually, and how we see ourselves.

Jean: "Always Moving Fast"

In the four years before buying the house with Karen and Louise, I had a series of major life transitions: starting a business, becoming a grandmother, changing jobs, divorce after 39 years of marriage, moving from a house to a rental duplex, culminating with the move to Shadowlawn.

With much on my plate, I always move fast. I'm determined not to miss anything, especially opportunities for fun with friends and family. People come first. I most admire those who are independent, clever, have integrity, and are kind. I see myself as a nurturing people person, but I expect my friendships to be equivalent.

Ladies at leisure, from left: Karen, Jean and Louise

My work life is multi-faceted. I continue a part-time nursing career, while running a home-based business. I am concerned about social justice and the environment, interested in politics, and I contribute both my time and money.

Sometimes I bring all these interests and values together, as I did by merging poetry and song for a church program to raise awareness of the human injustices that permeate this world. One of my nursing specialties was therapeutic humor, a way to help others heal by helping them choose a perspective of humor and laughter to lower stress and reverse negativity.

I'm whimsical and practical, optimistic yet concerned and proactive about financial realities and security. My children and their families are primary. I invest time and energy only in what's important to me. Life is short.

I have an eclectic sense of style that includes a little country, some antiques, contemporary touches, some crystal, lots of pottery, fabrics for clothing and furnishings from batik to silk; all is governed by how it makes me feel. If an item brings a smile to my face, it's in. Our combined possessions create a pleasing effect in the common areas and I often find myself moving things to find the sweet spot. As often as not, someone else moves it back; such is life in a community.

Karen: "Elegance in Simplicity"

I've been called a study in contrasts. As someone who travels half my days for work, my life is structured and organized. Paradoxically, I'm a risk-taker who has chosen change, travel and adventure over a settled life. I never miss a beat for clients, but I sometimes neglect personal things, like meeting the deadline for our state's mandatory car inspection.

It's a matter of priorities, of placing the needs of others ahead of my own. I always help others, but my strong independent streak makes it hard for me to accept offers in kind. Louise and Jean keep trying.

I'm a techie. I enjoy the latest, best-designed equipment – which clashes with my desire to have a minimal number of objects around the house. (I joke that I'm going to "become a Buddhist, renouncing material cravings, just as soon as I have everything I want.")

My books reflect my primary hobbies: cooking, photography, reading historical fiction (with Dorothy Dunnett my favorite author), and gardening. I might take a month to research and prepare a garden for one rose bush, but the resulting roses will be extraordinary.

I am long-married, long-divorced. I love mentoring young people, including students during my previous career at a small college, and the children of friends.

Some friends call me "Mother of Beardsley" (the cat). Some who don't know me well have mistakenly assumed that Beardsley is my son. But she is a black and white cat named after Aubrey Beardsley, a British illustrator of striking, black ink drawings.

Aesthetically, I seek "elegance in simplicity." Having too much stuff around annoys me. So I ruthlessly apply my own guideline: if I haven't used something recently or it does not hold sentimental or financial value, I dispose of it, preferably by giving it to someone. I had just finished renovating my Sears Roebuck cottage to that standard, a perfect little place for one cat and me. But I never got to see my English cottage garden grow.

Louise: "Comfy in Her Skin" (Maybe)

Others think I'm "comfortable in my skin," but appearances can be deceiving. They probably assume I'm supremely confident because I'm assertive and opinionated. While prone to jump to quick conclusions, I also try to be fair-minded. People who know me have probably figured out that I need time to warm up to new ideas, but might eventually come around to their point of view, or at least compromise. While determined to do things my way, I can be flexible. Seeing my impact on others, I adjust accordingly.

One of my core beliefs is that people should speak up for what they believe in, even when it is difficult. I try to live my principles in practical ways. Like Karen, I'm very independent and resist asking for help, although I'm generally happy to help others when needed.

By profession, I'm a clinical psychologist, providing services to children, adults and families. I thrive on a busy pace but secretly yearn for more time spent reading or puttering in the yard and garden. I really love a good political or intellectual discussion – the more controversial, the better. And I'm proud of being a decent amateur singer.

Before moving to Shadowlawn, I lived alone happily for six years, post-divorce. My fast-paced lifestyle made me rarely home and never lonely. One day, it occurred to me that I might as well be living in a furnished room, not needing the space of the Cape Cod where I had raised my son and daughter, a crowded little house that I decorated with an eclectic, busy touch and lots of color.

Beardsley: "Feisty Feline Survivor"

There's a rule among our friends: no lengthy pet stories at social gatherings; they can get boring. But we'll violate the rule here, because this adventure would not have happened without Beardsley, a feisty, female black-and-white Tuxedo "mutt" cat with a chin spot goatee.

"B." is a survivor. More humanoid than cat (we know, everyone says that about their cat), she is moody as well as strong-willed. Although normally well behaved, Beardsley can be provoked…and provocative.

Here's a prime example. We remember it fondly, though it was infuriating at the time. Beardsley was banished to the outdoors during a fund-raising event because some guests were allergic to cats. But she sneaked back in and retaliated, dashing across seated guests' laps, dipping her tail in the whipped cream on their desserts, tipping a cup of coffee, and then disappearing almost before anyone knew what had happened.

Also lovable and cuddly, Beardsley began it all.

Beardsley: "Of course I did; all things revolve around me."

All things revolve around me.

FOUR

Blame It on the Cat

We three had known one another socially for many years, but weren't close friends. So what brought us together into this adventure in cooperative householding?

It's curious how a seemingly isolated incident can trigger a cascade of events that bring people together and change lives. The catalyst for creating a cooperative household was Karen's need to find a home for Beardsley, then 11 years old.

In the 1990's, Karen changed careers. For a while, she worked from home, but then found herself traveling more and more for work. Eventually, she was assigned to a West Coast project, where she could not take Beardsley. We were all present the night that Karen tearfully confided her tough dilemma:

"I've tried everything to find Beardsley a home: cute ads, serious appeals, asking friends, checking with the no-kill shelter. But even the shelter won't take her, because they can't find a home for a cat that old. I can't find her a home, I can't take her with me to live in a hotel or fall prey to the coyotes out West, and I won't just abandon her. I've run out of options. People seem to think I can always come up with ways to fix problems. Not this time. I absolutely don't know what to do. Tomorrow morning, I guess I'll call the vet and ask him what people do in a situation like this."

Louise spoke up. "Wait a minute. You didn't ask me. It's obvious. We'll do shared custody: I'll take care of her at my house while you're gone, and you can have her back when you come home. After all, it's just for a couple of months."

With great relief, Karen accepted. Beardsley was saved. Later that night, Karen's phone rang. Knowing that Karen does not accept help easily, Louise was calling to repeat the offer so there could be no doubt that she was sincere.

So Beardsley moved in and took over Louise's house. Definitely the alpha cat, Beardsley intimidated poor Peaches (Louise's cat), who virtually moved to the basement. As often happens, Karen's project got extended: one month turned into six, six months turned into a year, and Beardsley lived on, learning to cope with the shared custody transitions. When Karen was in town, Beardsley lived with her; when Karen was out of town, she lived with Louise. The living arrangements were fine with her, but it was mortifying to be stuffed into a cat carrier and driven to the other house, yowling all the way.

Meanwhile, Karen's travel yielded many airline and hotel rewards points. Knowing that Louise would never accept payment, Karen convinced her to use the points for a "free" trip to Napa Valley and San Francisco. It was on this trip that they began to forge a real friendship.

One year turned into two, then three, then five. Beardsley lived on, traveling back and forth between her two homes. The thank-you trips, now dubbed "Annual Beardsley Guilt Trips" for the guilt Karen felt about imposing on Louise, afforded many opportunities for the two friends to see how each handled a variety of situations, from good to disappointing to downright stressful. Among other surprises was their discovery that Louise was the pragmatist and Karen the romantic. (Most people would guess the opposite.) When you travel with someone, you get to know her.

And then, after 39 years of marriage, Jean and her husband separated amicably and divorced. At lunch one day, friends urged Jean to plan a special adventure to launch her new life chapter. It didn't take much to convince her to join Karen, Louise and another mutual friend for the Fifth Annual Beardsley Guilt Trip. By the end of that trip, we all knew one another pretty well. Beardsley had brought us together.

Joint custody: Louise and Beardsley

Entrepreneur at work.

FIVE

An Interesting Exercise in Planning

A planner by nature, Karen started to talk about retirement, even though it was many years away. Jean and Louise, also single, would retire at about the same time. Although we were aware of some options for retirement and senior living, none seemed just right for us. Feeling as young as ever, we considered ourselves "ageless." We all planned to live independently, in our individual homes, for years to come.

As three singles, however, we were starting to find the responsibilities of maintaining our residences burdensome. Looking forward ten or twenty years, we saw the burden of single householding becoming ever heavier. For example, while decorating and entertaining for holidays can be wonderful, it is a lot of work when done single-handedly. Hosting parties is marvelous, but the house can feel pretty lonely once everyone has left and the kitchen is stacked with dirty dishes.

We considered that the need for companionship might become greater with age. We toyed with questions like, *"What would happen if I lived alone and needed emergency medical help?"*

We began to realize that maintaining three separate residences for three individuals was actually inconsistent with our values: prioritizing people and relationships, and being environmentally responsible. The obvious choice would be to purchase a retirement home together. In no time at all, we jokingly began referring to our dream as "The Old Biddies' Commune." The joke, however, was just among us. Not wanting to raise concerns or create jealousies, we kept our discussions private.

For several months, we tossed around ideas. Just for fun, we began sketching our dream retirement floor plan. We even wondered whether our aging joints would "need" a Jacuzzi. More importantly, we discussed how much privacy we would need.

In those casual discussions, we learned a lot about our shared values. A high priority for all of us was for friends and family to see our home as a gathering place – warm and friendly, with interesting conversation and lots of laughter. But despite common values, we each had a different perspective as we headed into this speculative venture.

Jean's Perspective: "An Entertaining Pastime"

Living together with friends in retirement: a novel idea, I thought. I was living alone in a rented duplex, following separation from my husband. I had never lived alone before and was enjoying my independence and freedom. However, I had to admit that sometimes I felt lonely, and I certainly did not enjoy big chores like lawn mowing or snow shoveling.

I am a people person; I prefer to share life experiences with others. This retirement idea might be a great way to maintain my independence and, at the same time, share my life with kindred spirits. There could be no downside to sharing household chores and expenses.

We tossed the idea around every time we were together. We began checking the Internet for retirement sites and inputting our criteria for an ideal geographic location. We compared results, hoping to find the perfect place where all three of us could find peace and contentment in our "golden years."

I thought this was an entertaining pastime that would probably not come to much, but as our fascination grew, we began to look more closely at options for shared living in retirement.

Our explorations unearthed many intriguing choices (though for some reason, we still had not come across the networks of intentional communities). E-mails flew back and forth, sharing Internet links and commentary.

As far as we knew, there was no how-to book for our idea. We realized that we had to develop our own strategy, so we began formal planning. Our idea was to lunch together one Sunday per month and spend the afternoon brainstorming. We developed an agenda that included open discussion and sharing the results of the research each had done since our last meeting. We would use flipcharts and notes and assign tasks. We envisioned this process to be our initial community-building work, and anticipated at least a year of planning.

But, as it turned out, we had only one meeting, April 25, 2004. As you skim our flipcharts, reproduced below, you'll see that we were very serious about careful, long-term planning. We wanted to gradually refine our understanding of what this venture might look like. And we expected that we would learn enough about one another to know whether or not we should proceed.

Karen's Perspective: "An Interesting Exercise in Planning"

My new consulting career offered opportunities to stabilize my long-term finances as well as to see the world. Sometimes I worked in a popular location, like the Bay Area of San Francisco. Other times, it was a swamp along the Mississippi coast. I always did my best to participate in the culture and see the beauty of the area, sometimes while looking through my camera lens.

My work offered more personal lenses. I work for a company that is richly supportive by giving its employees feedback, both positive and constructive. In my first few years, I learned much about myself and about working with others. In particular, I gained a greater understanding of how others see the world.

These great gifts came with the phenomenal bonus of travel points for airfare and hotels that supported our Annual Beardsley Guilt Trips.

But, the more I traveled, the more difficult it was to maintain my home and friendships. I managed to renovate my little Sears Roebuck house by using the Internet to send digital pictures back and forth to my contractor. I found a wonderful house manager to clean, deal with the mail and take care of any problems that arose. (Imagine needing a house manager for a four-room house!) Hiring others to take care of my personal affairs meant that I could concentrate on friendships during the little time I was home.

This lifestyle started me thinking about how much I valued my friends and family. I realized that I had constructed a solitary world for myself, one where I was happy enough, but one that lacked the warmth and spontaneity of people living together.

I knew, as I planned ahead for retirement, that I needed to change how I was living. Household responsibilities would

Time and space for solitude. Shhh...

become greater and, at some point, more than I wanted or could manage. As is true for each of us, I would at some point likely not be able to live by myself. And, statistically, the odds of a second marriage were low.

For a few years, I privately mulled these matters, then gradually began talking about them with Louise and Jean. Our pursuit of a living community was deliberate, although planned for a much longer timeframe than the one that evolved. I simply counted myself unbelievably lucky to have found two people who were willing to explore the possibilities – even if they were initially just playing along.

I laugh at our first planning session. It was just like being at work: organizing, capturing, simplifying, encouraging. What a relief to find that we all took turns in that role, as we talked our way toward deeper friendship and community.

To give you the flavor of the meeting, we have reproduced our flipcharts exactly as we created them in that planning session. They reflect what was important to us in the beginning.

Flipchart # 1

What agreements should we make to ensure that we plan efficiently and effectively, and that we're still friends regardless of the final outcome?

▶ Voice our positive & negative views early & whenever they are on our mind.

▶ Be clear and comfortable with respect to money matters.

▶ Don't sign anything related to money matters until it is reviewed by a financial advisor and attorney.

▶ Protect each person's financial interests, especially for heirs.

▶ Don't step down in lifestyle.

▶ Purchase a house that is a good investment, i.e., with good resale value.

▶ Make sure the financial plan is strong; that we will be in a better financial position by doing this than if we lived individually.

Flipchart # 2

What is my idea of a good retirement life?

▶ Financial security

▶ One or more events per week with friends

▶ One community service event per week

▶ Involvement in my religious community

▶ Ample cultural activities: theatre, musical performances, dance

▶ Educational opportunities—programs, trips, courses for seniors

▶ A college community with a good theater department or conservatory that welcomes community attendance

▶ Travel

▶ Pleasing, but not luxurious, environment

▶ Good climate

▶ Safe living environment

▶ Time and money for photography (for Jean & Karen)

▶ Singing opportunities (for Louise)

▶ Good market area for retirement work (for Jean)

▶ Good medical facilities

Flipchart # 3

What Geographical Areas Interest Us?

▶ Not overly humid
▶ Within 90-min. drive to an airport
▶ Within 30-min commute by public transportation to a major city
▶ Reasonable, if not low, taxes
▶ Low pollution
▶ Good proportion of sunshine to rain

Flipchart # 4

What Will The Benefits Be?

▶ Saving money on bills: mortgage, utilities, appliances, repairs, maintenance
▶ Interdependence: having people to depend on
▶ Less consumption: one lawn mower, vacuum, etc.
▶ Nicer house than we could afford separately
▶ Share entertaining
▶ Share interests; new horizons; joint endeavors

Flipchart #5

What Living Space Do We Want?

▶ 3 bedrooms

▶ 3 baths, one per person

▶ 3 offices/private sitting rooms

▶ Dining room

▶ Living room

▶ Kitchen

▶ Living space separated from public space for privacy when visitors are using community space

▶ Pleasant outdoor surroundings

Flipchart #6

Questions to Answer Later

▶ Do zoning regulations curtail multiple, non-related individuals living in a single-family dwelling?

▶ How do we manage to continue our independent lives while living communally? For example, what happens with holidays?

Flipchart #7

Homework for Next Planning Session

▶ Jean: Investigate zoning regulations.

▶ Karen: Create a spreadsheet with all the variables we need to consider; look at co-ops and condos for suggestions.

▶ Louise: Get books on retirement communities from the library and summarize.

By the end of our first three-hour meeting, we realized that we had astonishingly similar retirement needs and goals. And then, suddenly, the obvious question stared us in the face:

If this makes so much sense for retirement, why not now?

Louise's Guilty Secret: "But I Really LIKE Living Alone!"

When Karen asked, "Why not now?" and Jean agreed, I was nonplussed. Sorry to say, I wasn't completely honest with them but went along with the idea because, well, they were my friends. I didn't tell them what I was actually thinking:

I really LIKE living alone. My little house is perfect for me. Imagine the amount of work that I would have to do to move after living here for 21 years. What an incredible accumulation of stuff to sort through and get rid of.

But, on the other hand, maintaining a house alone is really expensive. And I'm rarely here. It would be nice to split all those household chores and obligations.

I zigzagged back and forth about the "commune" idea. I didn't want to just say no, and there was a sense of unreality to the whole scheme, anyway.

Finally, I settled on denial as a handy way to resolve my inner dilemma:

You know what? It will never really happen. I'll just go with the flow till the idea dwindles away. We'll go to some real estate open houses, find that nothing suits, and that will be the end of that. Besides, I enjoy looking at houses.

Beardsley: never wanted for attention.

SIX

This is It!

O nce we asked that fateful question, "Why not now?" we
left the meeting with a tantalizing sense of adventure.
We figured it would take six to twelve months to research the
possibilities, but the project soon became irresistible: Internet
searches, classified ads, real estate open houses, drive-bys. All
were excellent ways to consider what we really wanted in a
house.

At first we were oddly pessimistic. For some reason, we
doubted that we could find a suitable house in our suburban
Pittsburgh hometown, where we wanted to remain for the near-
term. We assumed that a potential move was many months
away and not at all a certainty. While it still didn't seem real,
our shared "daydream" grew increasingly more vivid.

We envisioned the details, considering each person's needs.
Because Karen and Jean each need a home office, we would
have to find a fairly large yet affordable house. They both like
to cook and require an efficient kitchen; Louise needs a niche

Love at first sight.

for her piano and sheet music. All of us like to entertain, so ample space in the communal living areas is a must. Three bathrooms, and parking for three automobiles: mandatory. A pretty yard would be a plus.

More questions emerged. Should we consider an older home that needed work? Should we choose a more interesting house in a less desirable location to save money? We visited a few real estate open houses over the course of three weeks; none measured up to our dream of the ideal communal living space.

That is, not until one Sunday evening.

As we drove by some houses that were remote possibilities, we made a random left turn when Louise spontaneously said, "Let's drive down Shadowlawn. I've been there before visiting a friend and it is a beautiful neighborhood."

And there it was, a lovely 1930s brick colonial house with a small "For Sale by Owner" sign in a tree-filled front yard.

We could hardly believe our eyes. We immediately used a cell phone to call the number on the sign. No answer. We started to drive away, when Jean spied someone sitting on the side porch.

She popped out of the car and almost shouted, "Can we see your house?" When the surprised owners ushered us in, we entered with great anticipation. Not wanting to inconvenience them, we briefly explained our atypical situation. Mary, the owner, smiled as she said, "I think this house will work very nicely for you."

And, incredibly, it met every one of our requirements.

This old but charming three-story, five-bedroom home had three and a half baths, thus meeting everyone's office and privacy needs. We noted the serviceable kitchen, the large living room with wood-burning fireplace (with gas starter for convenience) and built-in bookcases for all our collections. The house had a big-enough dining room and small sunroom with a bay window overlooking the wooded back yard.

Adding to the charm were the original woodwork and hardwood floors, though dark from age and scuffed by dog claws. The remodeled basement game room was an added attraction that would provide space for guests and a play area for Jean's grandson, then-three-year-old Seth. The two-car garage and deep driveway offered ample parking space. Of particular interest, the second floor and the finished attic were configured into two suites (each with bedroom, office and full bath) and a large master bedroom with full bath.

During the tour, the three of us exchanged meaningful glances but not one word until, as we left, Karen stunned Jean and Louise by looking the owner in the eye and saying, "We would seriously like to consider making an offer on your house."

As we got back into the car, practically giddy, we shouted to each other, "This is it! It's perfect. I wonder if we can afford it?

Karen, I can't believe you said that to the owner!"

We quickly calculated and realized that, best of all, the asking price was less than the total we were paying individually for our modest single dwellings.

Karen: "Forget the flipcharts."

Jean: "Now it's real."

Louise: "Did I really say that I liked living alone?"

Beardsley: "Four toilets to drink out of."

Suddenly, we were putting together personal financial statements and consulting with professionals to make an offer on a wonderful house that met all of our criteria for communal living.

Jean's Reflections . . .

I took a step back. Do I really want to live with these two people for the foreseeable future? How much do I value my independence? Would I actually have more independence if I could share the responsibilities of maintaining a home?

How would they feel about my three-year-old grandson visiting, as I am the only grandmother? Could I make an appropriate financial contribution to such an arrangement? Would I be able to hold my own with two other very strong-minded women?

Then again, why should all three of us continue the financial and maintenance burdens for three separate houses when we could have a home that none of us could individually afford?

I answered the questions and knew this was an opportunity I could not pass up. Here was a chance to live in a beautiful home with two good friends whom I respect and trust. So, with some trepidation, I joined the others in one of the most stressful two-month periods of our lives.

SEVEN

Serious Business:
Money, Mortgages and More

We had found the house. Everything was right: location, floor plan, space, style. We were all walking six inches off the ground. In our excitement, we wanted to make an offer right away and then figure out how to pay for it later.

But reason prevailed; we knew we had to proceed rationally. We lacked the time and knowledge to manage a for-sale-by-owner real estate deal on our own, so we quickly contracted with an agent who agreed to represent us for a fixed fee that was much less than the usual percentage.

We also immediately contacted an impartial financial planner and scheduled a meeting four days after we found the house, four nail-biting days during which someone else could have purchased "our" house. Sometimes, it is very difficult to take the rational approach.

Pipedream or Possibility?

For the first time, we needed to cross privacy boundaries to reveal confidential personal information to each other: our complete financial pictures. By now, we were dedicated to the idea of communal living, especially because we found a house that was optimal for our cooperative household.

We were making a deep commitment, personally, ethically and legally, with trusted friends. So, we pulled our financial information together, sharing copies with each other and with the planner who would help us determine whether our grand plan was a pipe dream or a realistic possibility.

The planner carefully examined our three documents during a highly charged silence across his desk. His verdict: Yes. We absolutely could afford our dream house. In that hour, we three became a little closer, sharing sensitive confidential information, building community with each step.

We had also consulted our individual financial advisors during this time, each of them assuring us that the investment was sound and likely to be profitable. We had adhered to our decision to consider only properties in geographic areas that had a reasonable chance of being a good real estate investment.

We barely had time to toast the verdict, as our agent was scheduled to make an offer. After some negotiation and much anxiety, our offer was accepted that same evening. Our heads were virtually spinning: the elapsed time from our meeting with the financial planner to the acceptance of our offer was less than four hours. Now we really had something to celebrate.

But first, we checked township ordinances to be sure that we, a group of unrelated individuals, could legally purchase a residence together. We were initially apprehensive about the exclusions that we might find in local zoning ordinances, because we had heard rumors of an archaic (now discredited) urban myth about "brothel laws" that prohibit groups of unmarried women from living together.

Our real estate closing: But there are only two signature lines!

No Time to Celebrate

No time for celebration, as non-stop meetings continued: mortgage brokers, insurance brokers, and an attorney to hammer out the details of this major, and rather unusual, transaction.

We called movers for estimates. At first, we naively hoped to save moving costs by coordinating our three moves on the same day with one mover. Impossible. Other realizations overwhelmed us: two houses to sell and a lease to break; the contents of three households to inventory to determine what would go with us and what would simply go – and on and on. All while we continued to work at our jobs full time or more.

Caution! "Thar Be Dragons"

There were some disappointments, which may serve as a warning to any who follow in our footsteps. Namely, be very careful when choosing advisors, mortgage sources and insurers.

The financial planner advised us not to be concerned about

preserving our individual shares of the equity in the house for our heirs. He breezily advised us to write off that money. Perhaps it would eventually go to the last partner standing; his intent was not clear. This seemed to us to be irresponsible financial advice, so we ignored it.

We needed two mortgage loans, a larger first mortgage and a smaller second mortgage. This was a financially wise alternative to paying mortgage insurance, which would have been required based on the amount we needed to borrow. We met with a highly recommended mortgage broker, but he presented misleading information, failing to mention that his rates were so good (too good to be true) because he was selling an interest-only second mortgage loan. We would never have paid down the principle of the mortgage loan and would not have built equity.

Fortunately, we spotted the omission before signing. Hindsight tells us that we were right to reject his offering, considering that the sale of this type of mortgage contributed heavily to the U.S. housing/financial crisis to come in 2008–2011.

Our advice: be alert and cautious. Don't fall for marketing hokum when you are mortgage shopping, no matter how enticing. Take a look at this e-mail sent by our ingratiating prospective broker:

Karen, Louise, and Jean,

I wanted to say how much I enjoyed meeting the 3 of you on Saturday. I told my wife about your plan and she wants to meet you too. Anyway, I have good news: I found a rate of 6.25% for a Fixed-30 year mortgage and 5.75% for a Fixed-15 year mortgage.

Also, I wanted to let you know that the advertised rates in the newspapers are "unrealistic." We think this is a lie and is wrong. We are very competitive and don't like to mislead our clients. We try to always keep our promises and treat our borrowers with the respect and honesty that they deserve. So, I want you to know that I will be honest and upfront with the 3 of you and will give you a very competitive rate with customer service that is second to none. I thank you again in advance for your consideration and trust in me.

This self-serving language put us on alert.

We quickly sought the services of another mortgage company, having wasted valuable time. Applying for a mortgage with three separate financial situations and credit scores was particularly harrowing. We believe, but cannot prove, that the bar was raised higher than usual for our atypical mortgage application. Instead of pooling our assets and credit scores, we believe that lenders evaluated us as separate buyers; different, for example, from a married couple seeking a mortgage. We were advised by one mortgage broker not to mention that we were crafting a legal partnership for fear of scaring the bankers away, so we didn't mention our General Partnership Agreement.

A General Partnership

One of our major tasks was the rapid formulation of a legal document to protect our heirs as well as our individual interests.

After much discussion about our concerns, we met with a real estate attorney who helped us draft a General Partnership Agreement (see Chapter 9 and our General Partnership Agreement at the end of the book).

Details, Details, Details...

Homeowner's insurance is required when applying for a mortgage, as well as providing essential financial protection. At clos-

Relaxing out back.

ing, we had to present a policy equal to the house's value before we could take possession. After requesting quotes from several insurance companies, we found one that gave us a reasonable price, not only on the homeowner's policy but also on our automobile insurance in a multi-line package.

Each of us took responsibility to arrange one utility service for the new house. This was not as simple as it sounds. Telephone service was the biggest challenge, since we chose to keep Louise's residential number but wanted a different service provider. In addition, we needed to coordinate telephone and cable services. Jean runs a home-based business with a fax machine, and Karen has lengthy business conference calls. We also needed an answering system. We used the telephone company answering service at first, then moved to an answering machine with three mailboxes. (Somehow, this still confuses callers, maybe because they don't listen to the explanatory message.)

Hunting grounds for one happy cat.

During each step we often interrupted our work for quick conference calls. E-mail exchanges updated the progress on our moving-related tasks, with many observations – both humorous and outrageous – gleaned from our daily contacts. Reading these e-mails became a daily ritual before retiring to bed at night and upon arising in the morning. The daily information sharing and decision making created stronger bonds among us; we were beginning to feel like a cooperative household, even though we hadn't yet coined the term.

During this time, we started to receive mysterious "B-mails." It turned out to be Beardsley, sending surreptitious nocturnal messages. Although they came from Louise's e-mail address, they clearly spoke in Beardsley's voice and provided comic relief.

From: lmachinist
Date: June 15, 10:30:55 PM EST
To: Karen Bush
Subject: B-mail

Dear Karen,

Thank goodness you have finally come to your senses. You know how I hate being trapped in that tiny carrier box, year after year, carted back and forth between our house and Big One's house. Buying one house just for me to live in is the purrfect plan. 4 toilets! And a big back yard with a fresh crop of tiny critters…

From: Your Mighty Huntress, B.

P.S. Thanks!

Beardsley "helping" Karen do her work.

EIGHT

Moving: Time for Triage

Fitting three mature households into one: time for triage! We scheduled time for all three of us to meet at each of our houses to select items that could be used in our new communal living areas.

From multiples of the same item, we chose the newest, best, and closest match for décor. After all, five vacuum cleaners, 25 pie plates, three coffeemakers and toasters, eight couches, three dining room tables, upward of 200 wineglasses, three lawnmowers, and 18 crates of Christmas decorations might have created crowding. (Thankfully, there was only one chainsaw – Karen's, of course.)

The following e-mail gives a glimmer of what we had to contend with. Karen concluded that Louise has a "table fetish."

From: "lmachinist"
Date: July 1 9:44:30 AM EDT
To: "Jean McQuillin," "Karen M. Bush"

Subject: Re: Inventory
At 9:18 PM lmachinist wrote:

Hi, Partners,

For anyone who might be thinking about decorating and furniture arranging, here are some of my pieces.

Horizontal file cabinet-2 drawer
Glass-topped patio table
Piano
2 Red/green plaid wingchairs
Colonial red couch
2 Small wicker green and brown armchairs
Round table – adjustable height top
Antique 3-drawer dresser
Maple 5-drawer dresser
Antique gate leg table
Antique drop leaf table – rectangular
Teacart
White and glass oval coffee table
3-drawer campaign chest
3-drawer end table
3-drawer colonial style end table
1-drawer campaign chest end table
Maple dining room table
Antique occasional table with interesting trim
Wood/glass/rattan octagonal coffee table

I didn't even bother listing the multitude of motley bookcases— at least 7, 8, 9.

Louise

For this to work, we each needed to let go of some items that we cared about. The new house was large enough but not huge, and it did not have a lot of storage space. The biggest challenge fell to Jean, who graciously agreed that the dining room furniture and living room couch she loved just wouldn't fit and would be sold.

Personal Space Items (PSIs)

If "personal space items" sounds like a euphemism, it is. It's a nice way of saying, "No way!" Many items were dear to the owner but not to the taste of the other two. We confronted such items up front, calling them "Personal Space Items" or PSIs.

As we sorted through our belongings, one of us would say, "Oh that will look wonderful in your personal space," sending the message that, while it might be pleasing to the owner, it would not be welcome in communal living space. This humor diffused (or defused) a potentially sensitive situation.

What made for a personal space item? The definition was broad, according to taste or how well the item fit with the rest of the house. Take Louise's mirror, for example. It's a large mirror with hammered tin motifs extending well beyond the frame. While it didn't fit with our living room furniture (or with Jean and Karen's taste), it looks great against the blue walls of Louise's bedroom.

Another example, Jean's torchiere lamp is...um...exotic – just perfect in a dark corner of the downstairs game room.

Then there is the picture of a magnolia branch that Karen's mother painted. Not a masterpiece, but a painting that Karen saw every day of her childhood. Now hanging in a corner of her bedroom, it is a fond remembrance of a mother long gone.

There were no serious hurt feelings, and we moved forward

in the spirit of integration, determined to create a unique home that would work for three individuals with definite but distinct tastes. From time to time, when one of us admires something in a store or catalog, someone else might say, pointedly, *"PSI,"* and we get the message.

Each owner sorted personal items. An astonishing eight pickup truckloads departed from Louise's house alone. An amazing number of superfluous remaining items were sold at a combined garage sale at Louise's house, yielding the first deposit to our newly opened joint household checking account. Three truckloads of rejects went to charity resale shops.

Moving Three Households into One

We got several moving estimates, hoping to find a company that could transport us simultaneously in one mega-move. This turned out to be a fantasy due to scheduling issues and the plain fact that, no matter how much we got rid of, we all still had too darned much stuff. A simultaneous move would have been utter chaos.

So we used separate moving companies and moved on different days. There was no financial benefit to scheduling three moves through one company, anyway. We used colored sticker dots on boxes and furniture to indicate the destination floor at Shadowlawn. Years later, we are still finding those little colored sticker dots. Happy memories.

We are three different individuals, and our separate moves reflected our personal and life styles:

- Karen, seriously crunched by her travel schedule and her old house's closing date just two days before we took possession of our new house, had movers pack and store her household, stayed with Louise for two days, then moved to the house the day after the Shadowlawn closing.

- Louise had movers transport only large furniture. The rest of her belongings were brought by car, with help from friends and family.

- Jean packed her things in boxes with the assistance of good friends, using the movers to take the boxes and furniture.

We were grateful that the closing on Louise's old house was not until mid-August. This gave Karen and Jean a place to stay after they moved out of their homes, because – surprise – extreme August humidity prevented the polyurethane on our newly refinished floors from drying. Another three days, and we could move in safely.

Chaos reigned at Louise's. Her daughter, Sarah, was in the process of removing her childhood possessions, which were piled out the door of her bedroom and down the main hallway, creating a minefield that claimed at least one casualty. Carefully avoiding the piles, Louise broke her little toe running into Karen's suitcase, a very bad time to have a painful broken toe.

Thank goodness Louise's parents arrived the weekend after we took possession to help pack and ferry boxes. At the end of an exhausting day, they took us out for dinner, where Louise's father counseled, "Now, you girls be nice to my Weesie."

Bountiful stress, but mostly good, because we worked so well together. We developed the heady sense that we could handle anything that came our way, including carrying boxes and furniture up three flights.

On Louise's moving day, two truckloads of her furniture arrived. Try as she might, Louise couldn't figure out how to fit that one extra couch into the living room after the movers left. Fortunately, a friendly new neighbor helped her haul it to the curb to become someone else's found treasure.

Second floor bedrooms:
top – Karen's; bottom – Louise's.

Jean's third floor perch.

Mission Accomplished: Phase 1

So the move was finished. In retrospect, it seems impossible that we accomplished so much in so little time. Rather than the gradual planning we first envisioned, our timeline moved up by months if not years. Consequently, details we had planned to explore over time were forcibly addressed immediately.

It all worked because we prioritized tasks and respected each other's diverse styles. We found it best to be very clear with each other when anyone had a concern. We stopped long enough to talk everything through, but we were efficient and did not belabor the issues. When we had consensus or a majority vote of agreement, we proceeded. We developed an open, honest style of working together that continues to serve us well.

Sharing Privacy

Before moving in, we had already selected bedrooms. Louise took the master bedroom with integral bath because she does not need a home office. That left Jean and Karen to make the tough choice between two rooms with bath on the second floor, or two rooms with bath in the finished attic.

After several days of deliberation, Karen said, "I know which rooms I favor, but either would be fine with me. Jean, you decide." Soon after, Jean chose the attic space. It turned out that Karen preferred the second floor anyway, so everyone was pleased. If Jean had wanted the second floor, either Karen would have cheerfully taken the third floor, or they would have drawn straws.

This willing flexibility is key to creating a workable shared living situation. Obviously, choosing to live together in shared space means that each person will not always have things his/her way.

During unpacking, we defined property boundaries: items brought into communal space were for the use of our little community. For instance, soon after the move, Jean noticed a book from Karen's house on the living room shelf and asked to borrow it. Louise pointed out, "But Jean, it's in your library." And so it was.

However, much as we encourage sharing, we set limits. From the very beginning, we did not enter one another's private space (bedrooms, bathrooms and offices) without permission, a boundary that we have steadfastly maintained.

Survival Strategies

As we picked our way along our uncertain path, we developed our own survival strategies. Here are some ideas that we recommend to anyone following in our footsteps:

- Each participant must unfailingly do every task to which they commit. And we did. This confirmed to us that we were the right people, in the right place, at the right time.
- Your best friend will be humor, applied liberally.
- A clear vision of what life will be like together will sustain you. Even in the midst of planning and moving, we started to create shared traditions and a pleasant home environment. Karen bought a copper fire pit in preparation for fall nights on the patio. Louise came to evening meetings with choices of tablecloths for the round table that we imagined placing in front of the bay window overlooking the backyard.
- Plan an open house to introduce your new home to friends, family and neighbors.
- Meet over shared meals. It's an enjoyable way to accomplish two things at once.

NINE

A How-To for You: Taking Care of Business

If you venture down the path to shared living, we are glad to help by offering the pointers that we learned the hard way. So this is a how-to chapter for potential partners in cooperative householding.

Keep in mind that *we are not attorneys, or accountants, or financial advisers.* Our expertise lies in our personal experience and our ability to suggest what you should watch out for.

We figured out the questions and sought advice from experts. You should do likewise.

Covering Your Assets: Legal Agreements
Rabbi Harold Kushner, author of *When Bad Things Happen to Good People,* was right: awful things sometimes happen through no fault of our own. We can have accidents. Crippling or fatal diseases can strike us. We can lose our jobs. Accepting that premise allowed us to think through the legal agreements we

wrote in a way that has proven to be very useful. We entered our adventure with openness and trust, but also considered every pitfall we could think of. The list included:

- One person deciding to leave our community voluntarily, for any reason.

- Two people deciding that the third was not working out and seeking to have that person leave.

- The death of one or more of us.

- Financial disaster striking any of us.

- One person allowing strangers or relatives to move in without the consent of the others.

- Failure to meet financial agreements.

- Irreconcilable differences.

- Loss of individual assets and estates for our heirs.

- Financial instability of the community, should a member leave or die.

That's a scary list of ugly but realistic potential events. We tackled each, sometimes for several hours, until we agreed on ways to protect our individual interests as best we could. Next, we drafted agreements and questions to review with an attorney. Below is the gist of those agreements, which were eventually formalized in a general partnership with each of us as a partner.

Note that these agreements were right for us and for the state we live in, Pennsylvania. If you decide to create a cooperative household, you will need a similar but different set of agreements attuned to your unique group of partners and the laws of your state and municipality. We highly recommend that you review your agreement with an attorney and financial adviser.

Being Hardnosed: The General Partnership Agreement

It took four revisions to hammer out the essential points of this agreement with our attorney. We Partners (Karen, Louise and Jean) agreed to form a "voluntary association for the sole purpose of conducting all business related to owning and maintaining the house we purchased." Here were the key points we agreed upon:

- Each Partner will contribute an equal amount, at the time of purchase and in monthly installments, to pay the mortgage, taxes, and all other costs.

- Our monthly fees will be deposited in our joint checking account by the fifteenth of each month.

- All house-related investments and debts will be equally shared.

- Although each Partner has equal authority, no Partner can incur any debts on behalf of the partnership in excess of $2,500. (We realized that there could be emergencies that would require quick action on the part of one person, such as a fire or other disaster. However, we expected to make joint decisions on all routine matters.)

- No Partner may unilaterally transfer or sell her share in our community to another person. (However, if someone will be away for an extended period, she may sublease her space with the agreement of the other partners.

- If one of us chooses to leave, she must provide written notice to withdraw a specified number of months ahead of time.

- Similarly, if a Partner does not fulfill her financial obligation, the others will ask her to withdraw, in writing.

- If a Partner dies, the interests of the others are protected via small life insurance policies that each of us obtained, naming the other two as beneficiaries. That way, if one Partner dies, the others will not be thrown into financial emergency and will have breathing space to make new arrangements (find another Partner, refinance, or sell the house) while the deceased Partner's monthly fee is taken care of.

- If a Partner leaves voluntarily for any reason, she must pay her monthly fee for a grace period while the other Partners reorganize and find a way to buy out her share of the property in a specified, timely manner.

- Likewise, in the event of a death, heirs of the deceased will receive their relative's equity in the house (based on current market value) in a timely manner. Of course, personal property (furniture, jewelry, cars, memorabilia, clothes) goes with us if we choose to depart, or reverts to heirs.

- Overnight visitors: We defined a maximum number of consecutive days, and total days per year, that a guest may reside under our roof. There was provision for flexibility in extraordinary circumstances, but only with the written agreement of the other Partners.

- Irreconcilable conflicts: we hated to even consider this, but conflicts can arise in any group of people. We agreed to retain the services of a professional mediator for a specified maximum number of hours to help us address and resolve serious problems. Failing that, we would move to an arbitrator and accept the arbitrator's decision.

All that might seem pretty hard-nosed. We love one another like friends and sisters, and trust each other implicitly. However, a life-changing legal and financial commitment requires a rational, "left-brained" approach with no room for sentimentality.

We planned carefully, regardless of trust; actually, we planned as if we didn't trust and were prepared for the worst. Our prudent legal agreements freed us from doubt and enhanced our relationships.

> *Caution: do not place your future in jeopardy by committing to any cooperative living arrangement unless your Partners are solvent, responsible, and willing to make legally binding commitments.*

To further help you think through what to include in a General Partnership Agreement, we have included our full agreement at the end of this book. Keep in mind that the specific details we agreed upon might not be the ones that best meet your household partnership needs.

Understanding Property Deeds

In our state, Pennsylvania, deeds can be written for an individual or several individuals, married or otherwise. We learned of two types of deeds: tenancy in common and joint tenancy.

Tenancy in Common: Two or more people own the title to a piece of property. In the event one or more owner dies, ownership passes to heirs, not to the other owner/s.

Joint Tenancy. Two or more people collectively own the property. In the event one or more owner dies, ownership passes to the surviving owner/s.

We followed our attorney's advice and procured a Tenancy in Common deed to protect our individual assets (equity and property) during the life of the partnership, and, in the event of our death, for our heirs. In other words, as Tenants in Common, if one (or more) of the partners dies, the surviving partners (or partner) do not automatically inherit the deceased's share of home equity or the property itself. Your circumstances might differ, so we advise you to consult an attorney prior to making any commitments.

Negotiating the Sale

The house that we bought was for sale by its owner. We might have saved money by negotiating the purchase ourselves, without using a real estate professional. But we knew our limits, especially in light of the complexity of our unique situation. The flat fee we paid to retain an experienced real estate agent as our representative was well worth the cost in peace of mind and a good outcome.

Although our real estate agent did a fine job, we discovered that the mortgage brokerage made several mistakes on our deed and mortgage documents, probably because they had rarely (or never) encountered a transaction like ours. We really needed to be alert, educated, and proactive to avoid errors. Even months later, we needed to redo and undo some glitches with our deed and mortgage.

On the other hand, the bankers who held our second mortgage were more than helpful. (Since the purchase, we have been able to retire the second, smaller mortgage.) Once we explained our situation, they enthusiastically went the extra mile to help us. One of the perplexing difficulties was that bank forms contain lines for only two borrowers, not three, necessitating double forms. Nonetheless, only two borrower names appear on the correspondence we receive, like monthly mortgage statements and yearly tax statements.

We divide the mortgage interest and real estate taxes by three to claim our appropriate share of the deduction when we file our individual income tax forms.

Almost all of the professionals we worked with seemed interested in our novel lifestyle choice and have been helpful. (Except the mortgage broker who "failed" to inform us that he was offering an interest-only second mortgage, and the financial counselor who told us not to worry about protecting our individual financial interests in the house.)

We strongly advise you to get multiple estimates on every transaction or service, and to be knowledgeable and assertive in all business dealings. Be aware that individual credit scores are the basis for decisions by mortgage lenders. We have been much more successful in dealing with our mortgagees/lenders on our own behalf than when we attempted to go through brokers.

Calculating Our Fair Share

Before making our initial offer on the house, we calculated reasonable estimates of monthly and yearly total household expenses, using information from the seller as well as our own prior experience. Our list included mortgage payments, taxes, homeowners' hazard and liability insurance, utilities, routine maintenance, emergency contingencies, gutter cleaning, plumbing, pest extermination, window washing, food and cleaning products. An accurate-as-possible estimate was necessary to determine if each of us could afford her share of the ongoing costs of the household.

After totaling the items and dividing by three, we determined a set monthly fee that each partner must deposit into our joint household checking account by the fifteenth of each month. We were delighted to realize that, with costs split three ways, we could purchase some services, like housecleaning and lawn mowing, that we had not been able to afford individually in the past.

Our initial monthly expense estimate proved to be accurate; we have had to increase it only minimally in our years at Shadowlawn.

Don't Forget These

Items to include when determining monthly fees for cooperative householders:

- Mortgage and taxes
- Insurance: homeowners and liability
- Gas
- Electric
- Water
- Sewage
- Trash removal
- Telephone
- Cable, DSL, or dish
- Household supplies (light bulbs, toilet paper, etc.)
- Housecleaning services
- Groceries in common
- Miscellaneous household needs (new tools, paint, wallpaper)
- Handyman services
- Occasional costs:
  - Piano tuning
  - Pest control
  - Roof check and repair
  - Gutter cleaning
  - Chimney cleaning
  - Firewood
  - AC/heating maintenance

Deciding What We Don't Share

With the exception of a joint household contribution to support the two public radio stations that we all listen to, the local medical rescue team, the town library, and a few additional minor fundraising requests (i.e., solicitations by our neighborhood Girl Scout cookie sellers), we generally do not make group charitable contributions. Those are individual decisions for individual budgets.

Saving on Energy

Cooperative householding has allowed us to realize significant savings on energy expenses. Even in the coldest winter months when the gas bill seems sky high, we are spending far less for heat than we collectively paid in our separate houses. We calculate that total utility costs are approximately 1/2 of the combined total costs at our three prior individual dwellings. The savings are magnified by the fact that no one previously had whole-house air conditioning, but now we do. Needless to say, we use 1/3 the number of household appliances. First come, first served works fine for sharing the washer and dryer.

We love saving money, of course, but the resource conservation thrills us. We'll run some numbers for you:

In 2003, Louise's utility bills totaled $3,113 with no air conditioning and no cable; Jean's were similar. Utility costs at Karen's tiny but high-tech house were $2,800.

Total: roughly $9,000 for three modest residences.

Here is the bottom line: our 2005 utilities totaled $5,332 for a big old 4-story air-conditioned house, a savings of almost 50%.

Getting Insured

Obtaining fire and hazard insurance is required before obtaining a mortgage. We gathered estimates from five insurance companies before making a decision. This was time-consuming, at a time when there was no time to spare, but it was well worth it.

We discovered huge differences in estimates for fire, hazard, and homeowner's liability insurance. In addition, we had the option of purchasing automobile insurance on all three cars from the same carrier at reduced rates. As with all of our business dealings during the frantic two months between falling in love with our house and the mortgage closing, every transaction was more complex than we could have imagined. For example, before giving us rate quotes, each insurance company needed all the information on all three partners, which included credit reports, social security numbers, birthdates, driver's license numbers, and the VINs (Vehicle Identification Numbers).

Paying the Bills/Balancing the Books

We pay most bills online. Accounting records are both digital (computerized banking) and pen-and-paper in our joint checkbook. The biggest threat to a balanced checkbook comes from the debit card, but if we forget to enter a purchase, at least it will show up online. We keep a reasonable cushion for emergencies, like emergency replacement of the six-year-old water heater that gave out a couple of months after we moved in. (Don't they always?)

We have agreed that no major household improvements will be initiated until there is a sizable checking account balance. When/if a balance accrues, we'll look for an interest-bearing account for savings. We pay down the mortgage principle with extra payments when we can, saving on long-term total interest and increasing equity.

The checkbook is in a designated spot at all times, so each partner can write checks as needed. When a bill comes in, someone pays it within days. We are proactive about taking care of business, in large measure because we are determined not to let one another down and because, somehow, completing even mundane tasks just feels more exciting than it used to. Here's hoping the novelty never wears off. If it does, plain old responsibility will just have to take over.

Bringing Home the Groceries

Developing an efficient and equitable system to handle grocery purchases was one of the hardest things to figure out. We decided to follow a doctrine of "don't sweat the small stuff," because it would be too burdensome to track everything that everyone buys and eats. Solution: Every month, we buy three grocery store gift cards out of joint funds. In addition to apportioning our food budget, these gift cards support a charity that is important to us. (Five percent of the face value is discounted back to the participating charity through the grocery corporation's community program.)

We use the grocery gift cards for household provisions, even if we don't always eat exactly the same foods, or amounts of foods, each month. If one of us chooses to entertain, party groceries are bought out of personal funds. This system works for us, but it highlights an important bottom line: this kind of arrangement can only work if all partners are absolutely reliable, honest, and consequently able to trust one another. The need for honesty applies to sharing the checking account and debit card, as well.

We don't often sit down for a meal together, but when we do, it is lovely. Whoever cooks is not expected to clean up. Leftovers are fair game for everyone. When one of us comes home from work, or a meeting, or a rehearsal, or from the airport late at night, it is wonderful to find dinner wrapped and waiting in the fridge. This is never expected, never taken for granted, and, therefore, always special and greatly appreciated when it happens.

Crunching the Numbers

Let's play mental arithmetic for a minute. Think about your own situation. Get ready to multiply and divide. Meditate on your taxes, utility costs, household services, hours of home maintenance, kitchen staples, etc. – actually, any costs you want to consider. Divide by 2, 3 or 4. How could you use that extra money? Those hours?

Now, consider what you pay for rent, or the market value of your home. If you were part of a cooperative household, you could multiply that by 2, 3, or 4. How much would that enhance your lifestyle?

Estimating Your Resources for a Cooperative Household

The tables below will help you see the possibilities of expanding your resources through a shared living arrangement.

The first table shows you the funds that would be available just for housing if you combined resources with two other people. In the case of the low budget example, someone who currently spends $750 per month on housing would have $2,250-per-month for housing by sharing a place with two other people. The size and quality of housing could jump significantly. For example, a single parent living in a small apartment with a child might now be able to afford a house in a neighborhood with better schools. Similarly, someone in the high budget example could have numerous housing possibilities, including an option to spend less, save more.

Use the right-hand column to estimate your own funds. List your current housing costs in the top row. List the number of housemates planned (including yourself in the number) in the middle row. Then multiply your current costs times the number of housemates to get your potential total funds available for housing. Put that number in the bottom row.

Calculating Funds for Housing (Monthly)	Low Budget	High Budget	Your Budget
Current costs for housing: mortgage or rent + insurance + taxes	$750	$2,500	
Number of housemates planned	× 3	× 3	
Funds available for a cooperative household (current costs × number of housemates)	$2,250	$7,500	

Use the following table in a similar fashion, to calculate funds available for household expenses. Again, you will see that your resources expand well beyond your current budget constraints. You would probably have much more than you need. You will recall that we were able to cut our total utility costs by half.

Calculating Funds for Household Expenses (Monthly)	Low Budget	High Budget	Your Budget
Utilities: electricity + gas + water + cable; and other recurring expenses	$150	$600	
Number of housemates planned	× 3	× 3	
Funds available for a cooperative household (multiply current costs by the number of housemates)	$450	$1,800	

Making Budget Choices

Your calculations in the tables above can allow you to make a preliminary estimate of your budgets for housing and household expenses. Be excited by the possibilities, but keep your feet on the ground. Are you factoring in all expenses? Are you being realistic? If yes, then you are in a good position to think about an important choice:

> Do I spend or do I save?

With new resources opened up, you have new options. Think about the long-term value of saving some of your new resources. We did. And each of us will live far better when we finally retire than we could have if we had continued living alone in the interim – or if we had lived more extravagantly together.

Becoming More Self-Sufficient, Together

To save money together, we learned to do household projects that we didn't think we could handle, or at least had never bothered with before. Karen completely refurbished the screen/

storm doors and did a beautiful job. Jean graveled between the patio stones to avoid a costly cement job. Louise figured out how to replace the mantels in the "antique" gaslight, a yearly chore. We've all picked up a paintbrush, or re-programmed the thermostat, or changed the furnace filters. Sometimes, we feel like we can do anything – and sometimes we really can.

On occasion, we've kicked in personal money to fund a purchase or project that was important to one of us but wasn't a group priority. For example, Louise just can't seem to resist buying flowers to plant. She doesn't expect this excess to come out of household funds, knowing that everyone else is satisfied that we have enough. And only one of us wanted that nice new refrigerator…

Reality Check: Expect Glitches

We won't pretend that all of our taking-care-of-business efforts have gone well. Due to our compressed timeframe at the time of our house purchase and move, we quickly accepted recommendations from our real estate agent, family, friends, neighbors – nearly anybody – for services we needed to hire. Because the house was 65 years old, we opted to have an official house inspection. The report mentioned the aging furnace and hot water heater, but was otherwise glowing, especially about the original wooden shutters on the house.

We felt secure about our investment, until we moved in and noticed a few problems.

The first discovery was that those beautiful shutters were being held together by makeshift home repairs. A coat of paint, hammer and wire fixed them temporarily.

But the second discovery was that the fuse box was antiquated and in dangerously poor condition. We needed major electrical work.

Friends recommended Tom, an electrician whose work appeared to be excellent. His bid to rewire many old outlets, install a new box with circuit breakers and add an integrated fire alarm was a bargain. Although Tom started work immediately, he disappeared for days at a time to attend an unusually large number of "out-of-town funerals."

One day, we discovered an empty rye whiskey bottle in the eaves where he had been working. We all agreed: no drinking on the job. Fortunately, before confronting Tom, we noticed that the bottle looked suspiciously old. It was bone dry, no scent of rye about it. No wonder. Closer inspection of the label revealed that it was bottled in 1936 at one of the local distilleries that thrived during Prohibition. Mystery solved: the original builder must have left the pint. Good thing we didn't confront Tom.

However, we should have heeded our instincts. Years later, a different electrician discovered that the new circuit breaker box had never been grounded, a problem we immediately corrected.

The moral: take time to discern to the best of your ability, even when you don't really have time. Be sure that the people you hire have excellent references from trusted sources. Ask questions, lots of questions. Try to be objective, no matter that you have fallen in love with a house. Look closely. Put your hand on those lovely green shutters to see if they are solid. Hope for good luck but be prepared for glitches, because glitches happen.

TEN

Potpourri: Living in Harmony

The essential taking-care-of-business details that we've just shared with you create the legal foundation and the organizational framework that are essential to the success of our cooperative household. But the personal interactions and relationships that build on top of that structure are equally important. Because they are complex and intangible, constructing happy working relationships is much trickier than figuring out how to pay bills or buy groceries.

We all know this from life experience: sometimes it's the little personal habits that come between family members, close friends or partners in cooperative households. Even with the best of intentions, people can get on each other's nerves or get their feelings hurt. One of the risks, but also the richest reward, of life in community is close connection with others. But how can you be sure that you and your prospective housemates will hit it off?

We hate to say it, but, realistically, there are no guarantees.

Do the best you can ahead of time to chose wisely, based on personality, lifestyle and core values, but honestly, you really get to know people only when you live with them (think college roommates, military buddies, spouses, or overstaying houseguests).

We offer the following vignettes as a sample of how disparate householders can live in harmony, at least most of the time, and deal with dissonance in healthy ways.

There Goes the Closet

As we anticipated moving in together, we were all prepared to be tolerant and flexible and good humored. But there was a subtle hint of disappointment in Karen's voice on our very first day when she opened the coat closet door to discover that it already held 25 coats and 12 umbrellas (Jean's and Louise's) and was full to bursting. Karen laughed it off: "There goes the coat closet," and trundled her coats to another spot. The inconvenience was only temporary. We pared the coat inventory and installed a second hanging rod, doubling the space.

25 Pounds of Pasta

A large, mysterious carton had been plunked down right in the middle of the kitchen floor on Jean's moving-in day. Ripping open the box, Karen and Louise were astonished to discover the treasure trove it contained: Jean's pasta collection – at least 25 pounds, from spaghetti down to rotini, all from the kitchen of a woman who professed to be on a no-carb diet. We couldn't accommodate it all, even with a pantry closet. What to do? Jean split the goods with her daughter, Maureen. Her defense:

> *"The pantry cupboard I had just moved from was very deep. I didn't realize the amount of pasta I had. Wow!"*

Over-spiced: Who needs 3 jars of paprika?

The pasta cache was just one tip of many icebergs. We discovered that each of us had accumulated excesses in our areas of interest. Louise, with enough furniture and knickknacks for two houses, never buys food; in contrast, Jean keeps the fridge and pantry amply stocked.

And then there is Karen. Her housemates wondered about her tendency to have multiples of things. Buying in bulk seemed to contradict her preference for having minimal stuff. The first instance came to light after she had been up in her suite for many hours, unpacking and putting away. Appearing for dinner, she asked sheepishly, "Does anyone need any pens?" She had bagsful of pens, markers and highlighters numbering in the hundreds. She had also hoarded an impressive stash of computer cables.

Karen explained this embarrassment of riches: it was the logical result of always being on the road, living in multiple places at the same time, and not remembering to pack all that was needed. If one is in San Francisco and needs a highlighter or computer cable, one buys it.

From time to time, Jean and Louise still hear Karen asking a guest, "Do you need any pens?" It took at least two years to find good homes for that initial trove.

But wait. Karen's collections sometimes come in handy. On a lark, she had purchased the entire inventory of frames from a photography studio that closed in the 1980s. She culled 400 frames down to 200 that looked useful, storing them in her office closet. Now, whenever someone needs a frame, she is invited to "shop in Karen's frame shop." Already, the lucky recipients (Louise, Jean, Louise's mother and friends) have recouped the cost of these unique customized frames, which make beautiful gifts.

Clutter Counts

Clutter could make cooperative householding irritating for housemates who like tidy surroundings. On the other hand, neatness might feel too confining to those who prefer a cluttered, "lived-in" environment. This is why we suggest that every member of a potential housing partnership should visit each partner's home to check comfort levels before making a commitment. It is not likely that a person will change lifestyle habits after a move to a shared household. At least, don't count on it.

That being said, social expectations and consideration for the good of the group do make a difference. The three of us have modified prior habits to some extent. There was no reason not to leave things lying around when we lived alone, but now we just don't do it, at least not in shared space. And Louise has learned to see beauty in a tabletop free of excess knicknacks and doodads.

Territorial Animals

People are. Need we say more? Well, okay, we'll flesh it out with the reminder that sharing territory, resources and control is one of life's biggest challenges to human nature. But we can coexist peaceably, drawing on mindfulness, good will and self-control. A motto that helps:

> Our house, not just my house.

Excess Baggage

Knowing that one person's trash can be another person's treasure, each of us tries not to get defensive or take it personally when the others suggest storing or removing a prized possession. But when we see the need, we tactfully and respectfully suggest that someone might "downsize." Several charity resale shops have benefited from this.

Karen prefers open space and wants few objets d'art or plants that (she says) "attack" people as they walk by. Louise and Jean have learned to appreciate the beauties of greater simplicity.

Not every decorative item needs to be displayed 24/7. We cooperatively rotate "display privilege" so that some cherished treasures stay in a basement storage closet most of the time, emerging only on special occasions. (Examples: Louise's stuffed roosters, a rotund bust of Beethoven, and Jean's flamenco dancer statue.)

We threw a White Elephant Party for friends, who carried away our excess baggage and had a great time in the process. A brief period of "mourning" sometimes preceded letting go, but experience taught us that once something is out the door, it is forgotten. (At least until it surfaces again; see matchbook collection story, below.)

It is amazing how familiarity and a non-objective eye create unnecessary attachments. Letting go of excess possessions, and sharing most of what remains, has actually felt liberating.

> ## I am not my stuff.

There is a paradox we've noticed but haven't quite figured out. Each of us has strong aesthetic and intellectual tastes, and we are particular about our belongings and our surroundings. But for some reason, none of us tries to control the community space. It's probably because we know we can't be controlling if we want this shared household to work. We've kept an emotional even keel about things – at least so far.

We give each other permission to make some unilateral decisions. For example, when Louise and Karen went out to the movies one night, Jean suddenly got what we call a "decorating tic." She rearranged many of the pictures and decorative effects in the shared living area. After the fact, she nervously anticipated her housemates' reactions when she heard them coming up the steps three hours later. It was fine. Not quite Louise's way; not quite Karen's way, but fine. It was Jean's turn to take initiative. For significant differences of aesthetic opinion, we would have worked it out with consensus and/or compromise.

> ## Do your own thing, within reason, and keep good perspective on where that fine line, "within reason," lies.

"You Were There, Too?"

But then there was the matchbook collection accumulated over many years by Louise's ex-husband, complete with celebrity autographs inside the covers. Karen and Jean invited some friends over to help themselves to our excess stuff while Louise was out one evening.

Who knew that the little wrinkled brown bag filled with matchbooks was something special?

Louise didn't miss it at all, didn't even realize that it was gone, until she began to find celebrity matchbooks on the dinner tables of friends, including the one with "Batman" Adam West's autograph. She was astonished:

What a coincidence! I also have a matchbook autographed by Batman in 1972... You actually attended the wedding of my ex-sister-in-law in New York in 1980? I didn't even know you were there.

Well, we just didn't need 500 books of matches.

> Let it flow; let it go.

Priorities: "Here – Have a Key"

A few of our lifestyle differences have been important. We took them seriously and resolved them with mutual respect. For example, Karen and Louise handed out house keys like candy during the moving-in phase to enable repair people to come in while we were at work. But, for obvious good reasons, Jean was concerned about security. So we stopped handing out keys except where we knew someone well. And, eventually, we changed the locks.

Of course, habits are harder to change than locks. In some instances, it has been tougher to adjust little daily routines than to make major transitions. For example, some of us leave rinsed dirty dishes and silverware in the sink, despite others worrying about stuff going down the drain or getting broken.

Some changes really go against the grain. One of us uses a sponge for kitchen duty; two prefer dishrags. Tough as it is, switching from dishrags to sponges is nothing compared to the real biggie: under-handed toilet-paper-rolling vs. the "right way." We give each other credit for being considerate and accepting both a sponge and a dishrag, but the toilet paper must be over-handed.

For settling minor differences about house priorities, the democratic process works quickly, every time. We've put several issues to the vote: safety lighting beat decorative improvements; smoke detectors beat wallpaper; a water heater beat a new powder room sink. Once a decision is made, we go with it; no second-guessing. There are some inner battles to fight, but the process has been a good stretching exercise.

> It's not all about me.

Old Cats/Old Tricks

Beardsley the cat's habits are definitely the toughest to put up with. She insists on throwing up hairballs on the white throw rug; it's always the white one. She's prone to topple and break planters and vases in a mad search for water in exotic places. But even the aging Beardsley was flexible enough to change her diet after Louise consulted a veterinary textbook and suggested a "senior diet" for better digestion.

Despite her willingness to accept a new, richer brand of cat food, Beardsley has had great difficulty understanding inflexible, even intolerant, human dietary tastes.

From: lmachinist
Date: September 24 1:12:11 AM EDT
To: karen
Cc: jean
Subject: B-mail

Dear Karen,

The Great Huntress is happy, smug, and proud – and my little tummy is bursting with fresh, juicy mouse. But why did Quick One scream when she opened the kitchen door in the midst of my breakfast on the doormat? Did she expect me to share it with her? Didn't she like my choice? Is she a vegetarian? What's wrong with her?

Confused,
Beardsley

Don't Help, Please

In the early days/weeks of our cooperative household, we found ourselves being overly helpful, as in bending over backwards. Sometimes it was annoying to be "helped," because feeling capable and in control is very important to each of us, independent sorts that we are. We've learned to say, "Don't help, please," in a neutral tone. We try not to take it personally when efforts to be overly solicitous ("motherly") are rebuffed.

Who would have thought that we would actually annoy each other most by being too helpful? Consequently, we've come to realize that it is best to help only when help is really needed or requested. The tricky thing is that not helping can make the uninvolved person feel guilty, like we're slacking off or not doing our share. This is a good problem to have, if you have to have a problem living as a group. And the solution is easy. Just say, "Don't help, please. Thank you."

On the other hand, we have all helped each other tremendously, in meaningful ways, from day one. In fact, an emergency cry for help startled Louise from a deep sleep on the very first morning after we had all moved in.

"I thought I was dreaming," she recalls, hearing moaning and muffled calls of "Help, help...I can't get out of bed."

Rushing to Karen's bedroom down the hall, Louise was appalled to find "Karen the Invincible" immobilized by what turned out to be a disc problem, the result of hauling boxes the previous day. Louise offered a strong pull, and then a push, to get poor Karen off the bed, onto her feet, and on her way to the phone to call the doctor.

Less dramatic, Karen frequently gives skillful technological assistance to housemates who are not sufficiently computer literate, only occasionally rolling her eyes in amazement at what we don't know but really should. Mutual help comes in many forms. Jean and Karen were both there when Louise needed transportation, nurturing, and moral support through two surgeries and post-treatments.

From: "Jean McQuillin"
Date: April 19
To: Karen
Cc: lmachinist
Subject: Re: Louise/Friday

Whatever else Louise asks for, get Jell-O & popsicles & pudding. Maybe ice cream, too.

No problem, I can handle the transportation both ways on Friday. Of course there is an outside chance that you, Louise, will stay overnight 'til Saturday. I am assuming that you,

Karen, could provide transportation Saturday if needed.

Jean

It's convenient for all of us to have in-home helpers to accomplish life's routine necessary stuff, like automobile service drop-offs and pick-ups, etc., which are bigger logistical challenges for people who live alone. Because no one asks for too much help, it balances out perfectly.

Woman on a Mission

We found, right from the beginning, that if something needed doing, it got done...by someone. We have not had to assign chores, as we each voluntarily take on tasks that need to be done, actually resulting in an odd sort of competition. We have each adopted some recurring tasks. Jean cleans the cat box weekly, for instance, and Louise does the twice-yearly task of removing/replacing the house's 21 window screens. When a large one-time task needs doing, one person often steps up; Karen and Jean recently stripped, sanded and repainted two wooden storm doors, saving us hundreds of dollars. Perhaps if there were more than three housemates, it might be necessary to assign chores to avoid duplication and to be sure that chores get completed.

Each of us pitches in to take care of mundane daily tasks: cleaning up after meals, unloading the dishwasher, weeding gardens, taking out trash, replacing toilet paper in the shared powder room. We plan ahead to tackle some large chores or projects together, scheduling a time when everyone is available.

We have some oddly differing housekeeping priorities, which turns out to be an advantage. Tasks that one or two of us might totally overlook get accomplished by a "woman on a mission," who suddenly gets a "bee in her bonnet" about a pet project.

Many hands: Jean and Karen refinishing screen doors.

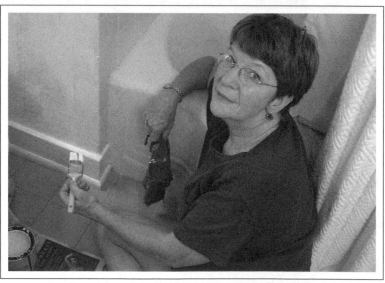

Sometimes we think we can tackle anything;
sometimes we really can.

Louise grapples with carpet tacks.

One evening, all three of us were sitting in the small sunroom, where we find ourselves congregating frequently. Karen suddenly noted that there were way too many cookbooks on the bookshelf, many of which hadn't been used in some time. She further declared that recipes can easily be found online and, if one really wants a particular cookbook, it can be downloaded for an e-reader. Before Jean knew what was happening, Karen, then Louise, were flinging most of their old cookbooks from the shelf, stuffing them into bags for donation to the library used book sale. Jean's reaction was, "Stop!" (She has not made the transition to electronic books; there is just something about the tangible item that she is not ready to forgo. She feels the same about the *New York Times*.)

The bee in Jean's bonnet was the patio stones in back of the house. The mortar between them was disintegrating, grass and weeds were growing up in the cracks, and something had to be done. We got estimates for a stonemason to remove and replace the mortar – hundreds and hundreds of dollars. Jean happened to be on a garden tour while visiting a friend in another city when she came upon similar patio stones with no mortar but small pebbles between the stones. Lots of elbow grease (Jean and Karen removing remnants of the old mortar) and a few bags of pebbles made the patio look great, and the pebbles are easy to maintain.

Louise thinks it looks nice but could hardly care less about that project. On the other hand, Louise goes into action in her own ways, like the time she suddenly "needed" to clean the basement windows, climbing into the disgusting spider- and slug-filled window wells in the back of the house and replacing the window well covers. One spring, Karen unilaterally took on cleaning and spray-painting all the patio furniture.

Once having seen the need for a project, any combination of one, two or three of us finds a way to make it happen. No need to nag or be mad at the non-participants, because our work contributions balance out over time. We all enjoy the results of each housemate's labor. We give credit where credit is due and, even better, offer a cold drink to the one who is working.

Woman on a mission. Who's making the cocoa?

ELEVEN

Creating Shared Community

Creating a functional community takes hard work as well as a big dollop of good luck. Our three lifetimes of relationships have taught us that interacting factors, working in complex combinations, determine the degree to which people can live together harmoniously. Even when everything looks positive at the outset, the ultimate test comes over time. Let's illustrate that heavy verbiage with an example.

Different People/Different Styles
Part of the adventure of cohouseholding involves learning to live with other people who approach situations in very different ways. Case in point: one Sunday evening after Jean, daughter Maureen, and son-in-law Mark had finished painting her bedroom, Karen and Louise offered to help clean up and put the furniture back in place. Jean protested, knowing that the others were as tired as she was. But they insisted, charging up the stairs to Jean's third-floor room with Jean on their heels.

As we returned a bookcase to its space, Jean noticed splatters of dried paint on the floor. Louise passed it off. "Oh well, it'll be under the bookcase and no one will ever know it's there." Jean disagreed, reaching for a wet cloth: "No, that's my floor and I want the paint to be cleaned up." But before that sentence was out of Jean's mouth, Karen was on her way to the basement to get the proper chemicals to clean up the mess.

This highlighted the differences in style among us. And it demonstrates how well-intentioned people can clash in a shared household:

- Louise is a "just-get-it-done person"– if it looks okay, then it is okay.

- Jean wants the problem to be solved, but will stop short of extreme efforts.

- Karen wants it done right and has a tool to solve most any problem. And she knows right where to find it; well, maybe.

In that paint-splatter moment of insight, we dissolved in laughter as we saw the future of problem-solving at Shadowlawn before us. Three different people; three different approaches. We say, "Vive la différence." However, it's important that we are all problem-solvers, with not a shirker in the bunch. We each have a contribution to make as well as much to learn from each other if we keep our minds open.

Expectations

We all know that unrealistic or faulty expectations can doom even the best relationships or endeavors. It's amazing how often people enter important relationships, including marriages, with the hope that the other person will change in some essential way to fit their partner's preferences. That change rarely takes place and is often the root of discord.

From the start, we tried to be very clear about expectations. But just what does that mean? Consider the various expectations that apply to our situation.

Mine: Our personal or individual expectations

Ours: Group expectations of the Shadowlawn partners

Theirs: Expectations of family, friends and neighbors

Some expectations are simple and easily met. Beardsley, for example, expects to receive unconditional love, attention and spoiling from all of us. But Karen is definitely in charge of Beardsley. She expects both Jean and Louise to follow her lead on matters of diet, outdoor privileges and medical treatment.

The neighbors rightly expect that we will maintain our property, and their property values, at least as well as everyone else in the neighborhood. And we do. But if they expect us to fit some type of neighborhood stereotype, such as one family to one house, they will be disappointed. And the lawn will not be perfect, which is very disappointing to the neighbor who accused us of "ruining property values" because of errant crabgrass. With a sigh of relief, we learned that he greets all neighborhood newcomers in the same gruff way.

Expectations held by family members are complex and multifaceted. Louise's mother expected and feared that *"three women can't get along in the same kitchen."* But so far, that hasn't proved to be a problem, likely due to differences in how we identify ourselves and prioritize what is important. As her mom knows well, Louise avoids cooking at all costs, so she is never underfoot. (To be fair, she makes huge batches of soup, spaghetti, potato salad or brownies several times a year to hold up her end, and often does the dishes.)

Our cooperative living arrangement prevents any of our adult children from assuming that "Mom's house is my house." Louise's son, Ben, and daughter, Sarah, have had to deal with the reality of losing their childhood home, the repository of much treasured stuff.

Realistically, we can't provide the same kind of "coming home to Mom's house" that Jean and Louise did in the past. But there are sensitive ways to allow each housemate to create a welcoming home base for her family members and friends, within reasonable parameters.

Jean's daughter, Maureen, who is married with four children and lives locally, expressed this best:

As a teenager, my parents' house was my house. I contributed nothing, felt entitled to total ownership of my bedroom, and became annoyed if the adults who also lived there asked me to pick up the things I consistently left strewn about the common areas. If the kitchen was not stocked with the free food delivered via shopping trips that other people made on my behalf, I did not stomp my feet, but I was certainly displeased.

In college, I would return home on breaks, and within minutes my coat would be draped over the banister, the fridge would be picked over, and my feet would be on the coffee table. It was quite an arrangement.

Once I began living on my own, my paradigm shifted only slightly. My parents' house didn't really feel like my house anymore, but I still felt it was my right to barge in unannounced, flop on the couch, and eat what I pleased. And let's be serious: my bedroom would always be the property of me.

In my twenties, my mom and dad moved to a new house.

I was perhaps a bit more respectful of their living space, but I still felt pretty comfortable that I could crash in the guest room and raid the kitchen at will. At one particular crossroads in my young life, I very easily negotiated free room and board for several months, and brought my indoor/outdoor cat.

Decidedly, everything completely changed after my parents' divorce and my mother's decision to move into a large house with two of her friends. At first, it was a little unnerving that suddenly there was no more "Hotel Uh-Oh" in case my life were to unravel. This place wasn't all Mom's house — it was also Louise's house and Karen's house.

One time, during a partial unraveling, I naturally assumed that I could stay at Mom's for a few weeks until I recovered from my drama at the time, but — gasp — I was declined! There was no clause for such an activity in Mom's residential agreement — this was no joke. This new house where my mother now lived was not my house.

As time passed, however, I discovered that knocking before entering someone's living space, waiting to be invited to a meal before eating, and hanging one's jacket in the hall closet wasn't really so awful. In fact, it's pretty reasonable. My visits to my mother's house are only slightly less indulgent than they were back when I declared myself the co-owner of her things. I even have a key to the house.

As it is, I feel very comfortable that I can walk around the house in my socks, snooze on the couch, and even snack from the pantry (although I don't expect anyone to keep me in mind on grocery trips.)

And, as if by design, when we are guests of my mother's, it feels as though she is the only one who lives there. Her housemates are either absent or exceptionally quiet, tucked away in their private spaces. When they do emerge, they usually are just passing through. They are always welcome and invited to join us, and sometimes they do, but they never assume and are always respectful of each other's time in the common areas with family.

Helping: Kitchen Wenches in Residence

At various times, we each expect to make ourselves scarce from family birthday parties, or to graciously accept a housemate's visitor or visitors in the basement family room/guest room, or to stay in the background but lend a helping hand on occasion. For example, when Jean's niece, Goldyn, had her wedding reception at our house, Louise was happy to play kitchen wench, washing numerous glasses and dishes that accumulated as the evening progressed. She chatted with the guests, mostly guys, who preferred to hang out in the kitchen.

Several family Christmas celebrations have occurred in the house, as well as Christmas dinners for "straggler" friends. The hostess always includes her housemates in the invitation, but sometimes each has separate plans. Housemates have joined relatives to open gifts on Christmas morning, and we have combined forces with extended family members and assorted friends for numerous festive holiday dinners. Family reunions include invitations to housemates, but we don't always attend.

If we're there to enjoy the dinner, we generally volunteer for kitchen cleanup duty afterwards. Having a "house staff" makes entertaining much less daunting.

For any event, we think about who will be with us and

Rare kitchen sighting: Louise makes meatloaf,
but she'd rather do clean-up.

how best to enable them to enjoy our home. There have been some challenging combinations of people. One year, Karen had invited a local "straggler" couple for Christmas dinner before learning that her family from California would be able to visit, after all. Except for the fact that all four are mature and gracious people, no two couples could have had less in common. In the days leading up to Christmas we wondered how we could keep everyone from getting into disagreements on politics, social issues and religious beliefs.

Our solution was to purchase a lighted lawn ornament in the shape of a deer – assembly required. It promised to be an excellent "guy" project to bring two male strangers together. We imagined how festive it would look in the snow in our back-yard. The day arrived, and we put the gang to work straight away. A few hours later, the deer was sparkling in the newly fallen snow and Christmas dinner was on the table. In honor of the two men who did most of the work, we christened that deer "Harry David." (And we enjoy the play on the name of the company that sends those ubiquitous fruit baskets during the holiday season.)

Each of us has declined invitations to social events in our house, usually citing an alternative activity or just staying upstairs in our personal space. It's important to allow each housemate to have private family times and, to tell the truth, we don't care to spend too much time within one another's family circles, no matter how nice the folks are.

As Karen put it, "I like your family, but I don't want to be part of your family."

However, Louise's dad sees it differently:

> *This has been a wonderful opportunity for these three ladies to upgrade their lifestyle at affordable cost. Best of all, old Mom and Dad received two lovely daughters in the process.*

Now "Dad" is the routine recipient of his favorite dessert, chocolate mousse, compliments of his "adopted daughters," who care greatly for him.

Early on, we confronted some awkward social situations with mutual friends who suddenly didn't know how to include one of us in an activity without inviting all three. We dealt with this, and will continue to deal with it, by frankly telling people that we are still three individuals, living individual lives, as before. After all, we are not a unit, though we happen to share the same address.

With good-natured ingenuity, our friends quickly created their own solutions. For holidays, one or more of us might receive individually addressed cards from mutual friends, as well as some mail addressed to "Jean, Karen, and Louise," or "Shadowlawn," or even "The O.B.C."

Drawing Lines: What We Are and Aren't

Being clear on exactly what you and your co-householders are – and aren't – is essential to success. In other types of arrangements, such as cohousing communities, senior citizen communities or communes, rules are generally spelled out to avoid difficulties and to set community standards. In our case, we haven't found a need for specific rules other than the provisions in the General Partnership Agreement.

Here is what we are not:

- **We are not** a marriage.
- **We are not** a family.
- **We are not** a business.

And here is what we are:

- **We are** a cooperative household.
- **We are** deed-holders under Tenancy in Common.
- **We are** co-mortgage holders.
- **We are** partners in a General Partnership Agreement that protects our individual interests and the interests of our heirs.
- **We are** close friends.

Perhaps just as important, we are all clear regarding the following:

- **We do not expect** to meet one another's personal needs for happiness or companionship.
- **We do not expect** to be dependent on one another, although we can totally depend on one another.
- **We do not expect** to change one another in any essential way.

- **We expect** that each of us will shoulder an equal share of responsibilities, although not necessarily the same degree or type of responsibility for each task.

- **We expect** that all will be sensitive and empathic about the reasonable priorities of each.

- **We expect** to follow through reliably with each of our responsibilities.

- **We expect** to share all items that are in joint space.

- **We expect** to ask, and to be asked, permission to enter private space or use private possessions.

- **We expect** to speak openly and respectfully about any and all issues that arise.

- **We expect** that we will not always agree.

- **We expect** that each of us is mature enough to handle whatever comes our way in a positive manner.

- **We expect** to work hard but to have a lot of fun as well.

- **We expect** that no one will talk behind anyone's back, either in or out of the house.

More on that final point: while we do minimize talking behind backs, each of the possible dyads sometimes mentions or even mildly grouses about the third party. Honestly, we believe this is simply human nature and we're stuck with it. We catch ourselves pretty fast, because we know that triangulating and forming alliances would be fatal to our community. Combining forces two against one is never a healthy way to create cohesiveness.

Unfortunately, one of our residents has displayed a nasty tendency to complain about the others through lengthy, secret "B-mails." These messages are obvious attempts to be ingratiating and manipulative. They provide a good/bad example of behavior to avoid.

From: lmachinist
Date: May 20, 10:30:55 PM EST
To: Karen Bush
Subject: B-mail

Dearest Karen,

It's been a long time, but this was my first access to a computer with no one watching. They keep things pretty locked down around here. But right now Big One is lounging outside on YOUR chaise, and Quick One is taking care of Littlest One, giving me a chance to get online.

First, about ME. My kibble is almost gone...the evaporated milk for my medicine is from cans that have been open for days...and Thursday night they left me outside grumbling and pawing the door for 3 hours while they were out.

And I saw Big One looking at your mail.

Beardsley

From: lmachinist
Date: May 21, 10:30:55 PM EST
To: Karen Bush
Subject: B-mail

Karen,

I'm aware that Beardsley has been at the computer surreptitiously again. I'm surprised that she didn't tattle about everything. Namely, your friends have decided that you are hosting a little party at your/our house on Friday at 7:30. Details later.

It is true that I peeked into some of your bills to see if payments are due, since you have been gone so long. Your automobile insurance is due June 8, but that's no problem 'cause you will be here in plenty of time. Another bill arrived from Verizon...

Safe travels home,

Louise

Setting Boundaries, Not Rules

It's a truism that all healthy relationships require healthy boundaries. Likewise, functional communities depend on functional boundaries. We're talking about personal boundaries, as defined in Wikipedia, for example, as "guidelines, rules or limits that a person creates to identify...reasonable, safe and permissible ways for other people to behave around him or her, and how he or she will respond when someone steps outside those limits." One might imagine tiny but strong psychological fences, fences that help to "make good neighbors."

Some of the ideas in this section overlap with the earlier discussions of "expectations." The crucial questions we want to consider in greater depth concern how, when and where to establish those personal boundaries. Awareness comes first; honest communication second.

We can offer many examples of boundary setting, some as simple as, "I can't talk; I have to work," or "I'm going to bed now." Figuring out how and when to interact with each housemate's extended family also brings boundary questions into play.

While each of us has happily volunteered to play occasional kitchen helper/cleanup detail for one of our housemates' social events, no one assumes that housemates are responsible for helping to entertain. Sometimes we are invited to an activity hosted by a housemate and we don't lift a finger. How delightful! When someone is entertaining, she is in charge. Here's the challenge: to let her simply do it her way, without "helpful" suggestions.

Once again, we simply can't stress this point too much:

> ### Successful cooperative householding depends on keeping good and solid boundaries.

By keeping healthy boundaries, we are respectful of each other. Supporting each person's independence and competence is affirming for all. No need for enablers; we are all strong and we celebrate each other's strengths.

People seem to be surprised that we have found no need for formal household rules. In our experience, responsibility, empathy and those all-important good boundaries suffice. To illustrate, if you happen to be the person who's home when the mail arrives, just bring it in and sort it, no matter that you have done the task every day that week and your housemates haven't taken a turn. But don't hold their paycheck envelopes up to the light to try to read the numbers inside. And don't ask, "Who's that from?" if you spot a mysterious personal letter.

Running low on eggs? Don't worry about whose turn it is; just pick up a dozen on your way home from work, and don't complain that someone ate "more than a fair share" from the last carton.

Remember to use your good common sense and disappear, after a friendly hello, when your housemate arrives home with a date. No peeking; no quizzing.

Have we said enough about that "B-word" already? Okay – let's move on to letter "D" and one more essential ingredient for happy cohouseholding. Coming right down to it, perhaps the bottom line prerequisite for success is self-discipline, in the best sense of the term. Good self-discipline requires knowing where important boundary lines are and then having the discipline to stay on the right side of them.

Bite Your Tongue

Living together inevitably fosters a climate of fraternal (or sisterly) intimacy – a natural mix of companionship, concern, compassion and curiosity. So it's important to figure out when to express comments, questions or opinions, and when to be silent. Even solicitous questions can come across as intrusive, especially when someone wants to deal with an issue privately.

Some questions are neither kind nor helpful, but merely reflect plain old curiosity or nosiness. For example, *"Who was on the phone?" "Where are you going?"* or *"When will you be back?"*

One of the nice things about living independently is not having to answer to anyone about your timetable or other details of your daily routine.

> Rule of thumb: We never checked up on each other before we moved in together, so no need to start micro-monitoring now.

Soon after we moved in together, a couple of commonplace incidents made us scratch our heads and think, *What should we do?* For example, Jean slept in later than usual one morning. Karen and Louise wondered, *Is she dead? Should we call up the stairs, or even go check?* Answer: No.

One night, Louise went to a movie after work and came

home at midnight. Jean wondered, *Should I call the police? Should Louise have called home?* Answer: No.

Karen had an early appointment, but Louise didn't hear her alarm going off in the morning. *Should I wake Karen to ask about the appointment?* Answer: No.

While it can be hard to know where the boundaries belong, gut feel seems to be the best guide. Plus talking it out, because your gut might feel different from mine.

Of course, sometimes housemates really do need to know each other's plans, because they directly impact others. Realistically, there are situations that would cause others to worry about safety. For example, if one of us is going to be away all night, we inform the others. Generally speaking, however, we each live our lives and conduct our private business as we did before.

> **If I have no need to know your business,
> I mind my own business.**

Communication: Open and Honest

It's sometimes tough to be open and honest, but we manage to take a deep breath and "fess up." When Jean backed her car into Karen's car, she took care of it immediately. When the plumber extracted the cap that had jammed the garbage disposal, Karen instantly said, "Uh. My fault. That's the little cap to the blender that I was using."

Because we feel terrible when it happens, it's hard to tell each other that we have accidentally damaged a cherished item. For some reason, Jean's breakable heirlooms seem to be the most vulnerable. Sometimes the guilty party is the cat, who has jumped up on a shelf. Other times, it's one of us moving an object clumsily.

Despite the discomfort, we force ourselves to tell what happened and we do our best to fix the breakage, sometimes sending items for professional repair or replacing a broken item with a new one. For example, Jean's porcelain statue of Martha Washington now has a little glue seam on its wrist. But you can barely notice that her Japanese earthenware tea glass has been glued back together.

Decision-Making: From Dilemma to Done Deal

Here's a happy surprise: so far, most of our group decisions have been unanimous, like when we all immediately agreed on the cherry floor stain and the need for electrical renovations, especially an integrated smoke detector system to provide early warning to Jean on the third floor.

If only we could always agree about everything; wouldn't that make life easy? No point fantasizing about it, because it can't happen. If any two or three people always agreed, something would probably be wrong. When we have differing decision-related opinions, we go to Plan C ("consensus") or Plan D ("democracy").

"Plan C"

Consensus decision-making is a group decision-making process that seeks the consent of all participants. To arrive at consensus means finding an acceptable resolution, one that can be supported, even if not the first choice of each individual. The process includes and respects all parties and generates as much agreement as possible, setting the stage for greater cooperation in implementing the resulting decisions.

It was our intent that by having each partner own an equal share of the house and contribute equally to household expenses, we would each have equal power. This does not take into account the fact that there is more than one form of power, however. For instance, personal style, level of self-confidence, the amount of information an individual has about the topic at hand, or level of passion about a particular issue – all have impact on the amount of power each person has in a given situation. We view power, or the ability to influence others, as a good thing. Positive power can benefit the group if used appropriately when building consensus.

"Plan D"

We manage some decisions by simply putting the issue to a quick vote. Two of us, voting together, constitute a majority opinion; the third allows the democratic process to rule. (Two votes over one vote wins. Pretty simple, right? There's the beauty of uneven numbers.). Generally speaking, each of us has been able to accept the majority decision graciously when the vote hasn't gone our way.

However, sometimes a particular issue has special importance to one of us, invoking strong personal feelings. Voting would give us a decision, but could result in lingering resentment or hurt feelings. In that case, we make the effort to find consensus, a more time consuming but ultimately more satisfying option because it honors the importance of all the participants, both their opinions and their feelings.

And Sometimes We Just Compromise: From Dishcloths to Butterflies

We've all had to compromise when our choice doesn't carry the day; we can be briefly unhappy about it, but that is normal and not a problem. For the most part, everyone has been able to let the disappointments go without personalizing them, holding on, or brooding. On the few occasions when we have had to tell each other, "No whining," it's with a light touch.

Oddly, one of our thorniest disagreements, a subject of repeated intense debate, is Dishrag vs. Sponge. Louise and Karen can't understand why anyone would want to use a disgusting, germy sponge. (Jean: "*But they can be washed in the dishwasher or sterilized in the microwave.*") Jean can't understand why anyone would want to have a wet and germy dishrag draped over the sink and in the way during food prep. (Karen: "*But they can be washed in the laundry with the dishtowels.*") Although both a dishcloth and a sponge reside on our kitchen sink, no one has been convinced and no one has switched sides.

Occasionally, it's hard to accept compromises and defer to the will and wisdom of the group, or to play by the rules. Louise really wanted dining room wallpaper, but the others weren't quite ready. With hope for the future, she began checking out wallpaper patterns surreptitiously, until the afternoon that Jean answered the telephone to hear, "*This is Acme Interiors calling to let Louise know that the wallpaper books she ordered are ready for pickup.*" Jean's reply: "*All right, I'll be sure to tell her.*" Upon hanging up, Jean let out a whoop of laughter as she anticipated letting Louise know she was "busted."

Being caught red-handed was actually funny, although Louise was a bit embarrassed. She tried hard to explain her way out of it: "I was just *window-shopping,*" but had to admit that she hadn't played by the rules – we had made a democratic decision about group priorities, after all. No hard feelings. And, amazingly, it paid off. The realization that Louise had been researching wallpaper let Karen and Jean know how much she really wanted to revitalize the dining room with a change from drab brown and dark gold, so they went along, somewhat reluc-tantly, with her plea to repaper with an exotic butterfly pattern.

Louise is adamant that the butterflies are subtle, not obtru-sive. In her opinion, they tie in beautifully with the view of the backyard out the dining room windows. But other people have apparently noticed and remembered those butterflies. But-terfly gifts in many guises have arrived over the years: classy and tasteless, big and small, garish and inconspicuous, furry and smooth, handmade and store-bought, garments and ornaments, you name it.

Our first butterfly gift was from our buddy and handyman, Charlie, who taped a silk butterfly on a wire to the dining room ceiling. We don't know how long it hovered over the dining table before we looked up to discover it. Probably every circle of friends has its little in-jokes. We're tired of butterflies, per se, but not the camaraderie and good-natured joke gifts. As we write this book, a chocolate butterfly lollipop rests in our freezer waiting for just the right occasion.

Prudent Problem Solving

Even when all three of us agree that *something has to be done* about a situation, it is prudent to consider alternatives and consequences before taking hasty action. For example, while preparing for the open house soon after we moved in, Jean was cleaning artichokes and the peelings went into the disposal. When the disposal was run, it clogged, making the sink unus-able during the event. Yikes!

Of course, the show had to go on, and we dealt with the situation as best we could. The next day, a Sunday, we called a plumber, who advised that to reach the clogged pipe, we would have to cut into a wall in the finished basement, a huge expense.

Fortunately, we waited to get a second opinion from another plumber and the clog was resolved rather easily at a reasonable cost. Needless to say, no more artichoke peels have gone down the disposal.

Most decisions about repairs or renovations have been made jointly. Although our Partnership Agreement stipulates that a Partner can incur up to $2,500 on behalf of the others, none of us has felt that she wants to take that much solo responsibility for initiating a costly project. We typically gather information regarding contractors and estimates, consider the information together and come to a decision.

Sometimes, there may be stronger interest on the part of one or two of us about the specifications of a particular job. For efficient management, one Partner usually takes lead responsibility for an individual project, getting referrals, gathering estimates, and overseeing the job, based on time and availability, with the others stepping in to help as needed during the actual work.

Case in point: we had some landscaping done on a day when Karen was working alone at home. Seeing that the contractor had delivered and was ready to plant 10 shrubs that had not been ordered, she called Louise and Jean at work to confer about what to do. Louise and Jean told her to make the decision she felt best, and we were all pleased with the outcome.

> **Decision Making Tip:**
> Don't belabor the issue; get it done.

Cooperative Endeavors

In any organization, community bonds are established and solidified through shared endeavors. The three of us happen to share many common interests and aspirations. Some of our joint activities dovetail with individual hobbies or interests. We share subscription tickets for music and theater companies that we all like. Jean and Karen are faithful supporters of Louise's semiprofessional choir. After many entreaties, Karen finally allowed Jean and Louise to select several of her finest photographs to frame and display in the living room. The housemates loved poring over her massive photo archives in the process. We trekked to the store, chose frames, matted, framed, hammered and hung them. Beautiful.

We are all strongly motivated to make our cooperative household work, now and into the foreseeable future, at the same time knowing that this is likely not a "till death do us part" kind of situation.

Sub-goals include transforming this old house into an attractive, warm, and welcoming place. A fun place. But it can't be done through unilateral action. And that's a challenging adjustment for adults who have run their own homes for a long time. We've had to practice patience versus impulsive action. We've had to work as a team or a trio. A collaborative style takes more time, but we haven't belabored the issues. Most questions resolve in a natural way, with a quick and easy decision.

We especially enjoyed these team projects: combining (with much discarding needed) three kitchens into one; entertaining friends on special and not-so-special occasions; adding new flowers and shrubs to the garden; developing holiday traditions; deciding on token birthday gifts to be enjoyed by all (flowers), and arranging an integrated library of all our many books.

And Speaking of Books...

In my/our/your living room library, the shelves are always bulging no matter how often we cull the books and pass things on to friends, book sales or libraries. It's an eclectic collection, from medical/wellness, to psychology/psychopathology, to humor and whimsy (many silly books about cats), all companionably leaning against heavy leadership consulting tomes on motivational interviewing and statistical analysis.

We cover poetry, photography, music, esoteric historical fiction, trash novels (no one admits to owning those but we all read them), and satire. Jean and Karen have thumbed through Louise's *The Little Book of Phobias* (Kohut) and *Affirmations for Cynics* (Thornbill and Wells). Of course, we own a shelf on cohousing and intentional communities.

Last, but certainly not least, our collection includes *The Bostonians* by William James. We mention *The Bostonians* because it has personal relevance. James' nineteenth century novel, considered provocative at the time, dramatized a two-woman shared household, presenting an alternative option to traditional marriage.

The term "Boston Marriage" was coined to describe shared living situations for independent single women, a very small, suspect minority at that time. When David Mamet's play, "Boston Marriage," was performed locally, we hosted a pre-play discussion of our own twenty-first century version. Questions and comments from the audience reflected interest and curiosity about cooperative householding.

Now, we move the story to our first Shadowlawn Christmas. It's where we made our biggest "mistake" to date. Who would have thought it would be over Christmas tree lights?

TWELVE

Blow-Ups at Shadowlawn?

Here's what people want to know. Over and over, people come right out with the irresistible question: *"Have you three ever had a fight?"* It's almost as if they are hoping we have, or maybe they just can't imagine how three strong-willed women can avoid major blow-ups.

The true answer is *No. So far, so good.*

Our closest call concerned, of all things, Christmas tree lights. Jean sent Karen and Louise to the local hardware to buy more strings of mini-lights while she cooked dinner. But in the throes of a brief nostalgia attack for the 1950s, Louise and Karen came back with the big, old-fashioned kind. They hadn't called Jean to confer about the sudden switch in plans, a small but pointed example of being inconsiderate. Jean was obviously unhappy, not just with the choice (she really dislikes those clunky lights), but mainly because she was left out of the loop.

The compromise: we agreed that the second Shadowlawn Christmas would feature small twinkle lights on the tree.

P.S. One year later: Louise was dismayed to find Karen and Jean stringing multicolored mini-lights when she had assumed white lights. Surprise – another communication glitch, but no biggie.

> Relationship Rule: No one gets left out.

Does our tree-light incident sound like a silly conflict? Louise's father, Ed, reminds us that in life and in relationships it is often "the little things that count." How many family fights are triggered by conflicts so insignificant that no one remembers what they were about when the argument is over?

Rationally, there is no need for divisive conflict, because there are multiple ways to compromise when people have the will to make it work. But human emotions are not rational.

Since we started our cooperative household, we've noticed that we are far less prone to vent emotions or to have conflicts/arguments with housemates than when we were with our own families in the past. What makes it easier to manage the emotions in our setting?

Louise thinks we work harder to stay on our "good behavior." Maybe we don't take things for granted, as one tends to do with relatives.

Oddly, the conflicts that have come closest to power struggles, causing stress and hurt feelings, have been gardening decisions. Gardening?

That might sound incongruous, but the gardens are important to each of us, and they reflect our different styles. Karen tends to keep only the best and replace everything else. Jean likes tidy gardens with space cleared around every plant so they have room to grow. Louise wants lots of color, a cottage garden jungle, and minimum weeding.

Tempers have flared (minimally, really) when cherished plants have been removed or too many new ones added with too little space. Maybe the time, money and physical work required add fuel to our frustrations. If someone has worked hard to achieve an effect that is not appreciated, it's easy to become snappish.

At one point, Louise even ventured to wonder if the others were being a bit passive-aggressive in the garden:

No sooner do I notice something really pretty in the garden than it disappears. What happened to the blue spiderwort? The daylilies in the rock garden? The white violets? The mahonia bush whose orange clusters in early spring were perfect against the blue forget-me-nots?

And sometimes, Louise just wants to relax, but the sight of Jean and Karen shoveling with gusto, digging out perfectly good perennial clusters to separate, cull and reposition, makes her upset.

Nothing gives me more inner conflict than when Jean and Karen are devoting yet another Memorial Day weekend to uprooting, thinning, and transplanting, when I really want to relax in the sun. I know I should just kick back with my book and cold drink. But not helping makes me feel guilty, and then I feel crabby. I complain to myself, 'Can't this gardening redesign ever be over?' I can't even concentrate on my book. Guess I'll just go to the backyard and plant these flats of impatiens quick as I can. I'll try not to notice what they're doing in the front garden. Later, I'll rescue those uprooted blue spiderworts and replant them right back where they came from.

So who's passive-aggressive now?

Karen and her giant lilies.

We actually discussed this problem over lunch. We brainstormed possible solutions like dividing up the territory, but we didn't seriously consider that. Instead, we settled for subtle compromises and adjustments. Our gardening priorities are different, because Jean and Karen really like to actively garden, celebrating the motto, *It's never done,* while Louise yearns to read a book reclining on a chaise while admiring the riotous blooms. Of course, the work is never done.

Peer Pressure?

Rather than digging in our heels when differences arise, we try to let ourselves be influenced by one another without giving up anything essential about who we are and what we think. We've mutually influenced each other in some small but surprising ways. We think it's a good way to stretch, to try things in different ways and to get out of one's individual rut or comfort zone.

For those who used to be more careless, it's actually nice to be neater. For those accustomed to eating beans out of a can while standing at the kitchen sink, it's nice to eat real home cooking. For those who are serious and strategic, it's nice to be frivolous and whimsical at times.

Perhaps we've grown better able to appreciate the beauty or usefulness of another person's take on life.

Shortly after moving in, sensible Karen told her housemates straight out that too much whimsy and kitsch just wouldn't appeal to her. She particularly feared that Jean and Louise would put tacky decorations on the two large statues of gryphons that flank our front door, offending the neighbors and embarrassing her.

Guess who adorned them with witch hats for Halloween, Santa hats for Christmas, and Mardi Gras beads and masks in season? Right...Karen.

Let it go.

Don't make it a job.

Life is good; enjoy it and share the joy.

But, What If....

People frequently ask, *"Do you think it would work as well if you were all retired and/or home all the time?"*

In our first eight years at Shadowlawn, Karen traveled routinely and often worked for extended times in other locations. In year nine, she worked from home more often before hitting the road again. When all three of us are in the house, it does change the dynamic, providing a glimpse of how things might be if we were retired. For one thing, Karen jumped into household fix-up projects with great gusto. Voilà! An updated kitchen.

Currently, we go our separate ways during the day and most evenings. We typically gather at the end of the day, on the rare evenings when everyone is actually home, to share thoughts and experiences and brainstorm ideas. We are all high energy, busy women. Even if we were retired, it is most likely that we would remain involved in a multitude of activities, according to our varied interests. We predict that our current routine, although perhaps more relaxed, would not significantly change. No crystal ball; just our best guess.

Definitely a 3-shovel / 3-shoveler snowstorm.

THIRTEEN

What We've Learned About Sharing from Sharing

As we toast the latest anniversary of our Shadowlawn adventure, we can say unanimously: *we are very happy with our cooperative household.* The years have flown by. In fact, working together as cooperative partners has been surprisingly easier than we expected.

Will it remain that way? Only time will tell. In life, changes and challenges are often unpredictable. At least we have control over how we manage the challenges that arise. So far, we have found each other to be fair and flexible, despite being strong personalities with definite opinions and preferences.

So, what have we learned? Lots. Basically, the building blocks of functional cohouseholding relationships come from life's general lessons. We like to think that, with maturity, we are growing wiser – not older – as our lives unfold.

How many people does it take to change the gaslight mantles?
Two to do the work; one to take the picture.

Shared Priorities Make Work Fun

We've had more fun doing household tasks than we ever did before, probably because we are not doing them alone or trying to coerce an unwilling partner to do unwelcome work. Fortunately, we share a similar level of motivation to create a comfortable, aesthetically pleasing home, so no one balks at the tasks (with only occasional exceptions.)

Internal motivation is the key to initiating action, even after a long day's work, when we sometimes get a second wind to do a domestic project. This is a huge change from past partnerships, when spouses were often on a different page. Certainly, none of our four collective husbands ever convulsed in giggles with us while hammering nails to hang pictures at midnight. Of course, not all women would share the same interests either; people have vastly differing priorities, unrelated to gender or any other category.

Here is something to think about before creating a cooperative household. Shared interests or passions are likely to increase mutual responsibility for the tasks of daily life and decrease conflict or disappointment among housemates.

Think ahead of time about the things that you and potential housemates might choose as the focal priorities of your home, and how those priorities would shape daily life. The list of possible shared, or possibly divisive, passions and/or interests is endless: children, extended family, wellness, music, cooking, entertaining, politics, sports, pets, reading, resource conservation, simple living, frugality, relaxation…whatever matters most to you.

Paradoxes, Risks and Rewards

Because we have shared motivation, we have hung together, literally and figuratively. If we can't do something alone, we can learn how to do it, call a handyperson, ask a neighbor, or wait for a housemate or two to help.

It's more personally fulfilling to participate in any kind of cooperative living arrangement when you don't expect other people to meet your physical or emotional needs.

When you aren't focused on getting your own needs met, generosity of spirit and caring connections grow and flourish all around.

The essential features that make our household work are not specific to us or to our situation. We believe that the same principles apply to any type of relationship, be it marriage, romantic partnership, friendship network, or family constellation.

Paradoxically, maintaining healthy relationships requires acceptance of an essential bottom line:

- Some differences between people are non-negotiable.

- Some behaviors are not acceptable.

- Some boundary violations necessarily will lead to the end of the relationship, or at least the end of the contract to live together.

Examples include a partner failing to contribute their agreed-upon financial share, abusing substances, being emotionally unstable, or failing to do a fair share of the work.

Once equilibrium is disrupted, codependency patterns and enabling can emerge (that is, one partner over-compensating for the deficiencies of another, leading to increased imbalance). Or conflict can erupt.

The three of us are very clear about the absolute boundaries. None of us intends to spend her time, energies or resources keeping someone else afloat who is not an equally responsible partner. Even if we could, we wouldn't. We've noticed that many women mature into a greater sense of self-respect and self-assertion over time, and so have we.

Here's another paradox: living together and sharing resources has improved our independent financial status to the point that no one needs to remain here for financial reasons, and each of us sees that we will be okay when we retire. When we do retire, we might go three separate ways again, although from our present vantage point, a once-again solo lifestyle is hard to envision.

No matter what the future brings, or how long this cooperative household lasts, we can be certain that each of the housemates has lived far better for far less than we would have in individual residences, thus saving more for the future. And we will hope to realize a good return on our housing investment, because we have been able to maintain the house and grounds responsibly, including capital improvements.

Sharing Essential Values

Shared living arrangements work most easily when the participants share *basic life values.* This type of compatibility runs deeper and broader than shared political, cultural or religious affiliation. *We're talking about a shared sense of what it means to be a good person, in relation to the world both inside and outside the house.*

> Basic values shape how we respond or reach out to the neighbors, their children, and the community beyond; how we allocate shared resources; how we negotiate with people we employ in the maintenance of our home; how we celebrate; how we support others in times of grief or trouble.

We realized that we were all on the same page when, a month after moving in, several neighbors' basements were flooded. Without hesitation, we offered a house key so that one of our new neighbors could access our laundry room whenever needed. This was a small thing, but a big thing, because it exemplifies how our little community interacts with and supports the larger community.

Environmental values also influence many choices we make, particularly household cleaning products, lawn care, entertainment and automobiles. Ethical and spiritual values determine which business people we deal with, how we deal with them and how we expect them to treat us, on down to those grocery gift/charitable donation cards we purchase each month.

We know that we could not have created a cohesive household if our individual lifestyle priorities differed significantly. For example, we have put major investments of time, energy and money into a pleasing décor, including the yard and gardens. Not every cooperative household would value or allocate significant resources to those things, which are objectively nonessential but important to us. If we weren't on the same page, it wouldn't work and would likely cause friction.

Many examples we offer in this book apply to us but not to everyone. We are sure that a satisfying and functional household could come in many forms, ranging from Spartan, simple, laid back and utilitarian, to highly structured, elegant, and luxurious. We are somewhere in between.

Here's a list of ten positive behavioral principles that allow cooperative householding to work:

10 Essential Behaviors:

- Self-observe and be self-aware.
- Be flexible as well as fair.
- Practice empathy for others; be kind.
- Maintain responsible independence.

- Communicate clearly, truthfully and respectfully.
- Do everything that you say you will do.
- Remember the "B-word." Respect good boundaries every day.
- Take care of yourself and be well.
- Maintain friendly optimism.
- Enjoy the adventure.

Expanding the Circle of Community

When we broke the news about our house purchase to a circle of good friends, Judy looked crestfallen. "Now that you'll be together all the time, I probably won't get to see you as much." Her fear was probably based on experiences with married friends who become so involved with their spouses that they reserved little time for friendships. In our case, however, cooperative householding had the opposite effect: we seem to have a greater sense, even a mission, of inclusivity.

Sharing Thanksgiving with family and friends.

Stockings were hung by the chimney with care...

Perhaps it's because we are a small friendship group and not a marriage that our attitude is "the more the merrier." We seem to entertain more often, and to initiate more group activities, than most of our acquaintances. Our community-centered thinking has expanded. It's more common for us to invite other people (couples or singles) to join us for holidays or other special events that used to be family-only, before Shadowlawn.

Interestingly, it was the three Shadowlawn women who first organized the neighbors to petition the township for long-needed repairs to our dangerously-potholed street. It was a great way to meet neighbors, as we successfully spearheaded this neglected street maintenance project. On occasion, a car would slow as it passed our house and one of the men on the block would call out, *"Would you please do something about that new pothole that's opened up in front of my house?"*

Creating and Sharing New Traditions

Like every community, Shadowlawn has developed its own traditions. In our first year together, we agreed that we would not exchange birthday presents. Instead, "the house" would give a gift of flowers to the birthday celebrant, who would naturally place the bouquet in shared space for all to enjoy. *From you I receive, to you I give, together we share...*

The first Christmas in the house, we purchased monogrammed stockings, for three humans and one feline, and hung them on the mantel. We wanted to have our own celebration apart from celebrating with our families, so we decided to fill the stockings spending a designated, modest sum. Of course, we each contributed to Beardsley's stocking. We chose one evening during the holiday season to share a nice dinner and to open our stockings while sipping Karen's family recipe eggnog.

This has become a tradition that we look forward to. We keep our eyes open for the perfect stocking stuffers all year long. At random times, perhaps in June or September, one of us might announce, *"I got you a great stocking stuffer today."*

Holiday dinners call for traditional recipes. We've broadened our repertoire of wonderful food traditions, most notably because Jean's family always has mashed rutabaga for Thanksgiving dinner. (Who else even knew what a rutabaga looks like?) One festive Thanksgiving, our 15 dinner guests reacted with everything from delight to disgust when the steaming tureen was passed. John refused to even try it.

By the time we cleared dishes, however, he had heard so many compliments that he decided to try a small spoonful. The rutabaga was so delicious that he devoured a separate heaping dish prior to dessert. Poor John has never lived this down. His rutabaga saga has been transformed into a twice-told tale.

Here it is, just in case you want to try it.

Jean's Rutabaga Casserole

2 large waxed rutabagas, peeled and cut into 2-inch pieces
2 pears, peeled and cut into 1-inch pieces
2 tablespoons orange marmalade
1 teaspoon dried ginger
1/2 teaspoon salt
1/2 teaspoon freshly ground pepper (or to taste)

In a large pot, bring 8 cups water to a boil over high heat. When boiling, add 1 tablespoon salt and the rutabagas. Boil until almost soft, about 20 minutes.

Once rutabagas are soft, add the pears and continue to cook until tender. It's better to overcook than undercook. Drain the rutabagas and pears well and return them to the pot on stovetop, heating until dry.

Place rutabagas and pears in a food processor.

Add the marmalade, ginger, salt, and a couple generous twists of pepper. Purée until smooth. If the purée seems dry, add a tablespoon or so of orange juice.

Turn into a casserole dish and bake in a 350-degree oven for 30 minutes. (The purée can be made a day in advance and refrigerated, and then heated in a 350-degree oven for an hour.) Yields 8-12 servings as a small side dish.

Karen loves to create computer-generated menus for special dinners using, of all things, a translucent photograph of that "tacky" dining room wallpaper as the background. (Yes, you can see those garish butterflies flitting around, right on your menu.) Some guests take such delight in that special touch that they have collected the menus over the years.

Here is the menu for that Thanksgiving feast that included John's rutabaga initiation.

Shadowlawn
Thanksgiving 2004

Belgian Endive with Curried Pumpkin Mousse
Spicy Shrimp Dip with Crackers

Herbed Goat Cheese with Roasted Beeet
and Watercress Salad
Egg Twist Rolls

Roasted Turkey with Rose's Calabrese Stuffing
Cranberry Relish and Cider Gravey
Crown of Broccoli with Lemon Beurre Blanc
Creamed Onions
Jean's Mashed Rutabaga
Riced Potatoes du Joi

Apple Pie Senneway
Amish Pumpkin Pie Armstrong
Pumpkin Ice Cream Pie Larson
Coffee, Tea

Silton d'Affinois, Cheddar
Port

Our 2004 Thanksgiving menu on dining room wallpaper background. We thought it was *très élégante* at the time – typos and all!

It takes a community to carry Karen's first batch of holiday eggnog.

FOURTEEN

Seriously, Now

A cooperative household is a home. As in a healthy family, there must be some non-negotiable expectations, such as being safe from physical and emotional harm. In this chapter, we offer some "tough love" messages for you, if you are considering cohouseholding.

In our case, we happen to have a lot in common in many essential ways, including religious beliefs, race, politics, same generation, same basic lifestyle, and even musical preferences. We can't know to what extent greater differences would have created stressful challenges.

Before you become involved in joint householding, we ask you to consider potentially difficult situations, in which different opinions, backgrounds or lifestyles could create tension for you.

Difference Can Make a Difference

Religious differences should be discussed, especially if one of you is particularly passionate about your beliefs. For example:

- Christians, Jews, and African-Americans who celebrate Kwanzaa: How will you handle the traditional holidays at the end of the year?

- Muslims and Buddhists: How will you find a way to comfortably pray or meditate daily in a mixed-religion household?

- Religious proselytizers: Will you seek to convert the others?

- Nonreligious: How will you react to others' religious practices, beliefs and talk?

Similarly, differing political views can quickly polarize relationships and result in disagreements that extend into other aspects of living together. How would you feel if one of your housemates placed a political sign on the lawn without your agreement? Can you imagine a battlefield yard filled with competing political signs?

Social Life vs. Private Life

An overlapping circle of friends, in addition to separate friendship circles, has made socializing easier than it might have been if we had three completely different groups to accommodate at parties or gatherings. On the other hand, our total number of friends and acquaintances is pretty large, because we participate in a number of different activities and associations. As a result, we have a constant stream of visitors and social obligations.

Our first lesson regarding friendship circles came when we drew up the invitation list for the open house right after we moved in. We expected the combined list to be about 50 people. Imagine our shock when we realized that we had verbally invited over 100 people even before we had made the list.

A warm and welcoming place for family and friends.

Consider whether you and potential housemates have compatible social life needs and comfort levels about having people in your home.

Competing Lifestyles

Since the three of us have entirely different schedules and all still work full time, each of us has the house to herself occasionally, adding to the sense of privacy and independence. If you and your prospective housemates all have the same schedule, you may want to consider whether too much togetherness might become an issue. Be sure to think about how much space you need, and how much "alone time."

Pets, allergens, odors, colors, patterns, decorating preferences, cleanliness, neatness, noise level, taste in music, house temperature, personal hygiene, substance use, and gun ownership are among the many factors that affect your comfort.

Which ones are important to you and to your prospective housemates? What other strong views and preferences will come into play? How compatible are you?

Deal-Breakers → Don't Go There

Here is a list of deal-breakers — circumstances that we believe should prompt you to stop any work you are doing on a cooperative household. If any of these situations applies to you, or to anyone with whom you may want to share a house, then run, don't walk, in the opposite direction.

- Substance abuse/addiction (alcohol, illegal drugs, food, gambling, compulsive shopping, sexual addiction).
- Uncontrolled medical condition.
- Financial instability/irresponsibility.
- Unmanageable significant other (ex-spouse, child, other).
- History of violent behavior.
- Serious legal problems.
- You view this person as someone who needs your help.
- You view this person as someone who can save you from your situation.

This list might seem harsh. But a cooperative household, as we envision it, is not the place for giving or receiving therapy for psychological problems, for recovery from substance abuse, or to regain financial or personal stability.

Under the right circumstances, cooperative householding offers a fabulous opportunity for reasonably mature, stable, independent adults to share community, resources, space, responsibilities, fellowship, and maybe even a feisty old cat.

FIFTEEN

An Informal Quiz: Is Cooperative Householding For You?

Since you have read this far, you may be considering your own version of cohouseholding. Maybe you would like to share community and resources with friends or relatives. If so, we encourage you to pursue your idea.

The first step is to decide whether or not cooperative householding, as described in this book, really is for you. So we developed a quiz to help you decide. By the end, you should have a pretty good sense of whether cohouseholding is for you. Or not.

The situations posed in the questions are hypothetical; most do not reflect challenges we have faced. (For example, none of us has an "alcoholic daughter" or a romantic partner who stays overnight every weekend.)

The questions are not based on scientific research. They should not be used to analyze people or as a test to pass. They merely stimulate you to think seriously about whether or not cooperative householding will work for you and others you might consider living with. There are no "right" or "wrong" answers, and sometimes more than one answer will fit your householding style.

Our hope is that by thinking about these questions and discussing your answers – especially differences in answers – you will be in a better position to decide if, how, and when to create your own cooperative household.

How We Created the Questions

We considered the values and personality/behavior characteristics that have helped us be happy and productive throughout our cohouseholding adventure: flexibility, agreeableness, appropriate social interactions, give and take, assertiveness, acceptance, fairness, positive outlook, honesty, openness, emotional balance, sense of humor, kindness, respect, reasonableness, keeping perspective, helpfulness, generosity, adaptability, communication.

And then we designed the questions to help you self-assess on these essential qualities.

The Quiz

Here are scenarios you might face in a cooperative household. For each, note the letter of your best response. How effective do you think each option would be for handling the situation with housemates?

1.   You like to eat meat several times a week, and you keep packages of steak and lamb chops, purchased with your own money, in the freezer with your name on them. The meat keeps disappearing.

a. You stew about who might be stealing your food, but keep replacing it in hopes that the problem will go away.

b. You call a meeting of your housemates to discuss your problem and possible solutions.

c. You are sure you know which person is taking the food and you tell him or her to stop.

2. You have lived quite compatibly for a year with two other housemates. One of your housemates develops a romantic relationship and is dating. Soon, the love interest is staying overnight every weekend and lingering over breakfast on Sunday mornings.

a. You stay in your room until noon every Sunday to avoid the unwanted guest.

b. You ask to discuss the problem of the unwanted guest to find a mutually agreeable solution.

c. You begin to invite your own guest to spend the nights and stay through weekend mornings to teach your housemate how inconvenient it is.

3. The powder room is old and it smells. All the housemates agree. A bathroom renovation is costly, and there is not enough money in the joint checking account to pay for the work.

a. You accept the undesirable powder room as a given, due to the financial situation, but you hate using it and complain.

b. After discussing the problem, you all agree to chip in some private funds to help pay for the renovation.

c. You choose to pay for the renovation yourself, and then resent your housemates' using the room.

d. You accept the smelly powder room with good grace.

4. One of your housemates has a four-year-old grandson who comes to visit regularly. You are concerned that the child will enter your private space.

a. *You keep your bedroom locked whenever the child is visiting.*

b. *You discuss with your housemate your expectation that the child will be told that private space is off limits.*

c. *You sternly tell the child that he is not to go near your bedroom.*

5. One of your potential housemates has a daughter who is addicted to alcohol and has no job. You know that this daughter has regularly asked for, and received, money, shelter and legal assistance from her parent.

a. *You say nothing, confident that your friend will make sure that the daughter's alcohol problem will not interfere with your householding agreement.*

b. *You choose not to go forward with entering into a householding agreement with your friend.*

c. *You tell your friend that you will only live with him/her if he/she forbids the daughter to visit your shared home.*

6. The fall season brings the weekly task of raking leaves. You care nothing about a neat lawn.

a. *You promise to help but never get around to it.*

b. *You discuss minimum standards that all can agree on and reduce the task to raking once every other week.*

c. *You hire someone to do your share.*

d. *You refuse to participate.*

7. Your housemate has not been paying the designated share of household expenses on time.

a. *You feel sorry for him/her and lend the money.*

b. *You repeatedly explain why failure to pay the bills is a problem and that you can't cover his/her share.*

c. *You allow the bills to pile up, waiting for him/her to chip in.*

d. *You ask him/her to leave for violating an essential aspect of the contract.*

8. **Your housemates do all the grocery shopping, but they don't get some of the brands you want.**

    a. You complain that they don't buy what you want.

    b. You specify brands you like on the household grocery list.

    c. You go out and buy the items you want.

9. **One housemate's family lives on the other side of the country. They come for a four-day holiday visit at a time when you enjoy being in the house with your own family.**

    a. You insist they stay in a motel.

    b. You join them for some activities but maintain your own family traditions and celebrate at the home of a relative who lives locally.

    c. You go out of town, after locking your door.

    d. You go out of town. You invite the housemate's visitors to use your bedroom, after you clean it up first.

10. **A mutual friend of everyone in the house invites just one of you to go to dinner and a movie.**

    a. You ask if you can join them.

    b. You feel hurt and assume that the other two don't like you.

    c. You go on with your life because it has nothing to do with you.

    d. You think that's a great opportunity for the two of them to have time together.

11. **A housemate always leaves dishes in the sink.**

    a. You rinse the dishes and put them in the dishwasher, saying nothing because you don't want to be pushy or hurt feelings.

    b. You leave the dishes alone, but don't like it.

    c. You begin leaving your own stuff in the sink.

    d. You discuss reasonable standards of neatness.

12. **You frequently find a light left on.**

   a. *You are annoyed but don't mention it for fear of your housemates calling you compulsive.*

   b. *You discuss your concerns about conservation and economy with your housemates and ask for some changes.*

   c. *You recognize that sometimes people forget, so just turn off the lights and don't let it bother you.*

13. **Your joint checking account never balances.**

   a. *You know which housemate messed up the checking account and confront him/her.*

   b. *You find out about online banking services to increase accuracy.*

   c. *You make sure that you are accurately using the checkbook yourself*

14. **A housemate is leaving personal items in the shared space.**

   a. *You ask him/her to remember to take belongings to his/her personal space.*

   b. *You put his/her stuff in the basket for "things to be taken upstairs."*

   c. *You throw the things in the trash.*

15. **You hear your housemate having an argument with someone on the phone.**

   a. *You consider the conversation to be private and act like you didn't hear it.*

   b. *You tell your housemate that you couldn't help overhearing the tone of the conversation and ask if he/she wants to talk about it.*

   c. *You ask your housemate what the argument was about.*

   d. *You tell your housemate that arguing in that tone of voice never gets anyone anywhere and offer suggestions for getting along better with people.*

16. Your housemate loves to read; you don't.

   a. You resent his/her silence.

   b. You try to get him/her to talk with you while reading.

   c. You develop a quiet hobby to pursue companionably in the same area.

   d. You go elsewhere and do something independently.

17. You are out of town a lot, so your housemates have to do most of the housework.

   a. You agree with your housemates that you will contribute extra money for them to hire help for housework.

   b. You feel happy you are getting out of it.

   c. You criticize what the others have done when you return.

   d. You say nothing, even though they have made major household changes without asking what you think.

18. After a very long week at work, you are relaxing in the family room doing a jigsaw puzzle, while watching a football game. You hear one of your housemates start to clean out and reorganize the storage area.

   a. You ask your housemate if he/she needs help with anything.

   b. You immediately turn off the TV and go to help.

   c. You continue to do your puzzle and watch the game.

   d. You tell your housemate that you're not going to help this time, because you need to relax, but will do a fair share of that, or a different, task later.

19. You are reading in bed. Your housemate comes in uninvited and plops down for a chat.

   a. You put your book down and talk, even though you are annoyed.

   b. Afterwards, you put up a "Keep Out" sign on the door and keep it shut.

   c. You remind your housemate to knock or ask to come in before entering.

d. You politely say that you want some private time to read and would prefer to talk another time.

20. **Your housemate smokes; you do not. Even though he/she agreed to smoke outside, he/she frequently smokes in the family room and kitchen; everything has a second-hand smoke odor.**

    a. You say nothing and live with the odor.

    b. You throw away the cigarettes and ashtrays whenever you find them.

    c. You say, "You are violating a house rule. If you are going to smoke, you need to go outside."

    d. You increasingly just stay in your room.

21. **Your housemate keeps music on constantly. You like quiet.**

    a. You ignore it.

    b. You ask him/her to turn it off, except when actively listening to it.

    c. You suggest that he/she leave the music on in personal space but not in the shared space.

    d. You suggest they plug in headphones or use an iPod.

22. **It is important for you to have good relationships with your neighbors. You notice that a housemate is unfriendly and sometimes even rude to the neighborhood children, offending their parents.**

    a. You apologize to the neighbors.

    b. You try to make up for your housemate's rudeness by giving the children special treats.

    c. You invite neighbors over more and more often.

    d. You talk with your housemate about the impression you believe he/she is making on the neighbors.

23. You have agreed to share your financial information prior to placing a bid on a house.

    a. *You list your key assets and debts, but don't tell your housemates all your financial information because some of it is embarrassing.*

    b. *You draw up a list of your key assets and debts and review them with your housemates.*

    c. *You give your housemates keys to your file cabinet and say, "What's mine is yours."*

24. Two weeks before you are scheduled to close on your house, one of your prospective housemates informs you that he/she has lost his/her job and cannot contribute the designated share of the down payment.

    a. *You tell him/her it's okay and arrange to temporarily cover that share of the down payment.*

    b. *You cancel the entire arrangement.*

    c. *You work with the real estate agent and bank to postpone the transaction.*

25. You and three other people have been living together for four months. You walk into the TV room and find one of your housemates cleaning a small gun. You are opposed to having weapons in the house, but it never occurred to you to discuss this topic before moving in together.

    a. *You demand that your housemate get rid of the firearm immediately.*

    b. *You scream and go to your private space, where you stay until you are sure the firearm is gone.*

    c. *You tell your housemate that having firearms in the house is unacceptable to you, but that you want to figure out a way to accommodate the need for having it.*

    d. *You ask the housemate to make some agreement about where the weapon will be stored, so you can worry less about it.*

26. You have found four other people who would make great housemates in nearly all ways. However, you differ in religious and political views. Three of you are very active in evangelical faiths; the other two have rejected religion and have negative views of churches. Two of you have very conservative political views; two are moderate; one is extremely liberal.

    a. *You decide that the differences in fundamental beliefs are too great to coexist peacefully. You abandon the idea of living together.*

    b. *You decide that the differences will offer great opportunities for lively debate. You quickly move ahead with plans to live together without discussion about religion or politics.*

    c. *You invite your prospective housemates to talk about how differences on religion and politics can help them or hurt them. You use that discussion to establish guidelines for the community.*

27. Certain soaps, candles, and perfumes cause migraines for you. Shortly after moving in together, one of your housemates lights a candle with one of the migraine-triggering odors.

    a. *You immediately extinguish the candle.*

    b. *You say to your housemate, "I'm sorry to tell you this, but I get migraines in response to certain odors. I wish it weren't so, but the candle you lit is one of them. Would you mind putting it out? I'd be happy to replace it with a candle that we both like."*

    c. *You say to your housemate, "That candle is giving me a headache. Please put it out."*

    d. *You close the door to your room, open the window, and take some medication to stop the migraine.*

28. **You are thinking of forming a cooperative household with three friends. You are about to place a bid on a house and are discussing the monthly budget. When you calculate the amount you will need to contribute each month, you realize that it will be a huge stretch for you.**

    a. *Proceed with the arrangements because you'll be able to live so much better.*

    b. *Tell your prospective housemates that you want to participate but their budget is too luxurious for you.*

    c. *Tell your housemates that you've decided you cannot be part of the plan.*

Your Turn Now

Develop your own questions, ones that reflect issues specifically important to you. For example, you might want to question and discuss issues of co-ed or multigenerational cooperative householding (adult parents with children, or adults and their parents) or potential personal hygiene issues, or laundry policies, or wellness, or... you name it.

As we said above, there are no "right" answers, but our experience has taught us that some responses indicate a greater willingness to live together and do what it takes to make it work.

So, how did you do? Did you select answers that show that you can:

1. Confront problems directly, rather than ignoring them or trying to get back at people?

2. Discuss situations openly, honestly, and with a neutral tone?

3. Make tough decisions that respect yourself and others?

4. Accept and live with democratic decisions without resentment?

If you can honestly answer yes, you might be a candidate for cooperative householding.

A rare treat – all at home at the same time,
zapping e-mails across the room.

SIXTEEN

Overcoming Barriers

Worry gives a small thing a big shadow.

SWEDISH PROVERB

In the Cooperative Householding workshops we give, at least one participant privately tells us something akin to: *"This idea makes so much sense. I'd love to do it. But you are all so bold and courageous! I would never be able to do what you've done."*

The first time we heard that statement we were stunned. We don't think of ourselves as particularly courageous and we don't recall having any significant fears. Concerns, yes. Fears, no. Yet we realize that the prospect of a life change as dramatic as creating a cooperative household could be very scary. It is important to acknowledge your emotional responses from the outset, as you start planning your version of cooperative householding. Let's return to the big question: is cooperative householding right for you?

Do It Your Way — Or Not at All

We've told you about our way. But our way might not be exactly your way. Variations on our approach to cooperative householding abound. Singles and couples could buy a home together. Single parents struggling to make ends meet could join forces to provide a much more comfortable living arrangement and community for raising their children. A group with a particular social interest or hobby could join forces. All sorts of arrangements are possible.

Before you start discussions with potential housemates, you need to answer a few questions for yourself. Even if you've taken the quiz in the previous chapter and feel you "passed" with flying colors, your views might change as you dive more deeply into options. To give you a framework for future discussions, here are three key questions to consider.

- What do you want?
- Do you want to live in a cooperative household?
- If so, what arrangements would suit you and what ones would not meet your needs?

All right, then, how might you decide what's best for you?

Go to Lunch

We offer you a technique that Karen has used when making life-changing decisions. Others have also found it a great way to think creatively yet practically about big changes. Her approach is simple: take a few people to lunch, one at a time, and ask their advice.

Here is how she suggests setting up the conversation so that it is creative, focused and helpful.

- **Choose advice-givers well.** They should know you well enough to give clear advice about your living arrangements, but not have any self-interest in your decision. Don't invite your sister, your child, or your best friend. Do invite someone who knows you well enough to know your likes and dislikes associated with lifestyle choices. That person might be a trusted coworker, a member of a community group you work with, or a spiritual adviser.

- **Set boundaries for the conversation** ahead of time and again at the start of your lunch. Here is a starter set for you to adapt.

  1. *I don't want to live alone and I'm thinking of starting a cooperative household where three or more people could live together to share resources and life in community.*

  2. *It will need to be a long lunch to allow for plenty of in-depth discussion – maybe two hours.*

  3. *I'll pay, because this is all about me.*

  4. *Give me advice and ideas, not sympathy, not empathy, not gushing enthusiasm. Hard, practical advice is what I want and need.*

  5. *Tell me what you think is good and what is bad about this idea – for me.*

  6. *Tell me frankly what I do well and not so well that would impact my sharing a cooperative household with other people.*

  7. *Who would be good housemates for me?*

  8. *Tell me what you think I should do. I will listen to your advice. I will consider it a great gift because it will help me make my decision. But know that I might or might not follow that advice.*

  9. *Everything we say in this conversation is confidential – on both sides.*

Acquaintances who have used this simple technique report that it generated some of the most memorable, positive conversations of their lives. They learned a lot about themselves. They left the conversations with fresh yet doable ideas, plus greater confidence in their ability to make a change. And each of them launched into a new endeavor – a career, a retirement plan, or even a move to a new location.

Be prepared, however, for a different yet equally good outcome. After listening to advice from your luncheon companions, you might decide that you are not cut out for cooperative householding. That's a fine outcome, too, because it will save you from putting time and effort into something that's not right for you. If that is the decision you reach, congratulate yourself and move on.

Meet Failure

Before we dive into the topic of committing to a cooperative household and overcoming barriers, here's a tip that we recommend to everyone:

> **Meet failure.**

We succeeded in creating a cooperative household that gave each of us more than we anticipated. But it could have been otherwise. It could have been a failure.

It turns out that each of us, in slightly different ways, considered what that would mean. So we invite you to mentally meet what failure would look like for you and to ask yourself the all-important question, *"If this cooperative household fails, will I be okay...can I still be happy?"*

Here's a way for you to address the prospect of failure, head-on. It involves writing down the ways in which your cooperative household could fail you.

Create some undisturbed time to sit in a quiet place. Be prepared to be honest with yourself. On a piece of paper, create a template with columns, as in the example below. We've listed a few of the potential issues that worry some of our workshop participants.

Type of Failure	Importance	Likelihood of Occurring	Prevention Plan
Financial disaster	High	Low	Share 3 years of federal tax records; agree on escrow fund; require two signatures on all checks.
Loss of contact with family & friends	High	Medium	Use the general partnership agreement to accommodate visitors.
Loss of privacy	Medium	Medium	Specify requirements for living arrangements.

Once you've got your template, start by listing the types of failure that worry you, how important each loss would be to you and how likely it is to occur. Last, write down what you plan to do to prevent that failure from happening.

Now, sit back and look at your chart. Highlight any line in which you wrote "medium" or "high" for importance or likelihood of occurrence. Consider those items non-negotiables for your cooperative householding agreements – items too important for you to back away from.

As you progress in planning your cooperative household, revisit the document you just created. Be sure that you are taking steps to prevent anything that could be a serious failure (and deal-breaker) for you.

Finding Your Prospective Housemates

Our workshop participants always ask about how to find the right people. Sometimes they come with a friend who is just right. They know each other well and they're up for the adventure, but they want a third or fourth person to join them. Sometimes they come by themselves and will need to find potential housemates, a task that can feel as daunting as finding someone to date or marry.

You, too, are probably wondering how you will find prospective housemates and how to be sure they are the right ones. We suggest that you start with some easy-to-do research, making a record of resources and ideas that are workable for you.

Here are a few suggestions for doing research:

- Go to your library, bookstore, or online and find one or two books on shared housing. Be sure to find ones that discuss long-term commitments, not just finding a short-term roommate. One excellent resource is Annamarie Pluhar's 2011 book, *Sharing Housing: A Guidebook for Finding and Keeping Good Housemates.*

- Network. Ask everyone you know what they advise for finding a trustworthy, compatible housemate.

- Use news media, especially blogs for "Boomers." Two active and informative ones are at AARP and The Huffington Post (HuffPost/50).

- Network some more. Sign up at www.meetup.com for groups in your area with similar interests. (Meetups are locally organized events open to anyone who has become an online member of the group. Most events are free or low cost.) Attend the events that interest you and think of all the people at that event as prospective housemates. You might even sponsor your own meetup and invite speakers who will help participants through the process of deciding what to do. (If you live in the Sarasota, Florida, area, go online and visit the *Living in Community Network*. They facilitate local meetups specifically to help participants find housemates.)

However you approach finding a housemate, rely on common sense. We've noticed that online matching services for senior shared housing opportunities have started to appear. These services charge a monthly fee and promise to find matches, similar to dating services. It is too soon to know how effective these services will be. So we simply recommend using some native caution if you pursue them. Similarly, placing an ad will cast your recruiting net wide and will generate unscreened responses. We recommend using an ad only if other networking has not panned out.

Going Forward

So you've decided to go forward and you now have a basic idea of what you want. Your next step is to explore options with a few other people – your prospective householding partners. One way to begin is to have those individuals read this book and discuss it. Ask some questions: What would be the pros of an arrangement like ours? What would be the cons? Who might truly be interested? How will you develop and honor the healthy boundaries we discuss? How will you know your deal-breakers and respect them without hurting one another?

You and your fellow explorers might want to read more about cooperative householding or the broader related topics of cohousing and intentional community. To help you find some excellent resources, see our resource pages at the end of the book. We also invite you to join us online, where we have discussion groups on various topics related to cooperative householding. You will find us at www.myhouseourhouse.com and at www.facebook.com/myhouseourhouse.

As you continue your explorations, here's a pattern to be on the lookout for, offered as a gentle hint: consider whether or not you want to spend your time talking and reading and talking and thinking and talking and... versus moving to action, even if it is just a small step.

Good first steps are to do some activities that approximate living together. Have meetings over meals at one another's houses and get a sense of how people live in their own place. Take a short or, preferably, a long vacation together. Deliberately do some things that will place stress on the group, perhaps completing a challenging hike (for team-building), or taking a low-budget road trip by car, or volunteering to work together for a week on a demanding charitable project. Think of your own version of a positive, yet stressful, activity. That experience will give you some idea of how the participants will get along for more than a few hours and if there are any issues that raise alarms. You might learn that you and one other prospective housemate love to cook or garden. Or that a prospective housemate lives in a house full of dog hair – something you can't tolerate. Or that someone who seemed aloof is actually very compassionate.

At some point, your gut will tell you that this is right for you or not. If it's not right for you, gracefully exit the group by indicating how much you have enjoyed getting to know everyone but that you simply don't want to continue the planning for a cooperative household. If it does feel right for you, formally invite some people to form a cooperative household.

Your Barriers: Are They Concerns or Fears?

Once you reach the point of knowing what you want and having good prospects for a cooperative household, your mind will probably swirl with a hundred questions and exciting visions of life in a great community. Some of your questions will pose barriers to creating your community and you need to address them.

One type of barrier is a **concern**, something that might be a problem but that can be resolved with more information. For example, if you are concerned about your ability to afford the costs, advice from a good financial adviser can resolve that concern. If you have concerns, you might be able to use the resources listed in Chapter 2 – Living Alone/Living Together.

Talk openly with your prospective cooperative householders about your concerns. Perhaps it would help to have each person form a list of concerns and discuss them, as we did early in our own planning process.

The second type of barrier, **fear**, is much more likely to stand in your way, so we will spend more time discussing it. By fear, we mean something that truly worries you – worries you to the point that it keeps you from sleeping, or you feel upset, anxious, or even queasy when you think about it. Fears are more difficult to address. The first steps are to recognize and accept that they exist.

To Fear Is to be Human

Anyone who has been around an infant knows that humans show fear from a very early age. Usually, those fears are irrational, but sometimes not. One infant we knew became stressed and cried when family members wore hats or even had their wet hair wrapped in a towel. Why? Did hats change the baby's perception of those familiar people into scary strangers? We'll never know; she was too young to tell us.

The relevant point is that fears begin early and life experiences teach us new ones. Those same experiences might – or might not – have taught us how to deal with fear.

Fear is a complex experience. Dictionary definitions emphasize that it is distress due to some sort of threat, real or perceived. Common antonyms for fear are courage, bravery. Were those workshop participants calling us courageous because we didn't share their fears about forming or living in a cooperative household? We think so.

We did have concerns, though, concerns that we have discussed in other chapters. But never did those concerns reach the level of fear that prevented us from moving forward. Why not?

Our friend, Carol, clued us in to a possible reason: we had each taken big risks before, and most of them had paid off. All of us have created change in our lives. We have left our family homes to go to school or to be with spouses. We have quit secure jobs and made career changes. We have left spouses with no firm housing arrangement in place. We have traveled, sometimes to politically or socially unstable places.

Our experiences taught us that change can be good and, to a great degree, that we were the primary determiners for making it a good change. We entered our planning and moving phases for Shadowlawn with a "can do" attitude. We believed that the upside would far outweigh the downside. On the flip side, if you have not made significant life changes, or have had painful change experiences, your fears are understandable.

Please don't think that we are trivializing these fears, but we just can't help pulling out one of Beardsley's classic B-mails to illustrate.

B-mail:

Dear K.K.,

I can't believe you are plotting to move again! And as usual I have no power and no say in the matter. Don't think I've forgotten some of those other awful times, like when you put us right on a main street with no hunting grounds, or when you deported me to live with Big One's pathetic white cat and scary children. I swore that I would never move again. So even tho' I'm kind of excited about that hoard of chipmunks under the patio, I'm going to fight tooth and claw to stay out of that d.... cat box when you try to stuff me into it.

Hssssssss

B.

Different Barriers for Different Folks

Here's a novel idea: we are not all alike! It's only natural that different people will have different concerns and fears about cooperative householding. Jean's concern involved holding her own with two other strong-minded individuals. Louise's concern was that she might be doing this for the wrong reason – to live in a house she loved. Karen's concern was that a group of three would fall into the childish pattern of two people being "in" and the third person being "out," thereby causing hurt feelings.

What are the barriers on your path to develop or participate in a cooperative household? Here is an exercise to help you identify your barriers and to determine which ones are concerns that can easily be addressed with more information and which ones are the real fears that require extra attention.

When you and your prospective housemates discuss a cooperative household, review the checklist of barriers below. If the barrier applies to you, check off whether it is a concern or a real fear that is blocking your move forward to forming a cooperative household. Add any that are missing from this list.

Barriers	This barrier is a...	
	Concern	Fear
Failure *What if it doesn't work out?*	❑	❑
Success *Who am I to take such a radical step and stand out from the crowd?*	❑	❑
Personal Failure *They won't like me after awhile.* *I'm no good at ...*	❑	❑
Uncertainty *They won't pay their share.* *We'll argue a lot.* *I know what I have now; I don't know what I'll have then.*	❑	❑
Moving *I'll have to give up things I want.*	❑	❑
Finances *I don't know if I can afford this.* *I don't know if they can afford this.*	❑	❑
Friendships *I'll lose my friends.*	❑	❑
Age or Health *I don't have the energy to do this.* *I don't have the health to do this.*	❑	❑
Knowledge *I don't know how to get good legal or financial advice.*	❑	❑
Privacy *I like solitude and won't get it.*	❑	❑

Barriers	This barrier is a...	
	Concern	Fear
Family *My family won't feel welcomed.* *I feel like I'm abandoning my son.*	❏	❏
Intimacy *What if I develop a romantic* *relationship? Will this arrangement keep* *someone from being interested in me?*	❏	❏
Compatibility *What if we don't like the same food?* *Movies? Level of music in the house?* *Cleanliness? Pets? House temperature?*	❏	❏
Trust *I don't really know how well I can trust* *these people.*	❏	❏
Other	❏	❏
Other	❏	❏
Other	❏	❏

You now have a preliminary list of what you will need to address before finalizing any cooperative householding arrangement. As we mentioned previously, you can address your concerns by gathering information and talking with people. But overcoming fears requires a different approach, if for no other reason than the emotional component of fear often keeps us from being rational.

Overcoming Your Fears

Although one of us is a clinical psychologist, we are not attempting to provide "how-to therapy." This section will simply provide some tips on overcoming the typical fears that each of us experiences from time to time as we contemplate change.

What can you do to overcome the fears you identified above? In part, that will depend on how you individually learn from and experience the world, a point we will return to. But despite individual differences in learning and coping styles, there are a few general tips that apply.

Understand Your Fear. Take one of the items you labeled as a fear. Write down what you are afraid of. Then answer the question, "What exactly do I mean by that?" Ask and answer that question four more times. For example, for a fear about compatibility, your answers could look like:

- *I'm afraid we won't get along.*
- *I'm afraid there will be tension in the house.*
- *I'm afraid that we will argue.*
- *I'm afraid that I'll back off of what I want or know to be right.*
- *I'm afraid that I'll be unhappy.*

Look at those answers. They practically cry out the solution! If you are truly afraid of arguments and tensions, you can form some agreements and processes, up front, on healthy ways to talk about differences that arise among household members – processes that ensure you are heard and respected. During your planning stages you can use those agreements. Either your group will use them and everyone will benefit, or your group won't use them and your fear was confirmed. It might be time to walk away.

Take Action. It's only human nature to think and talk about one's problems. That's fine. But the worst thing you can do is to dwell on a fear; you will only make it worse. Do something to confront it, change it or get over it.

The strategies that will work best for you depend on who you are. Most personality profiles describe four ways that people characteristically interact with other people and with the world we live in. So our tips for overcoming fears are grouped according to these four characteristics:

Fact Seeking tips empower the part of us that appreciates analysis, clear logic, and making decisions based on data and facts.

Problem-Solving tips empower the part of us that finds following a process or method to be a good way to find answers.

Social Connection tips empower the part of us that gains ideas and courage through personal relationships and interactions.

Intuition tips empower the part of us that ultimately relies on our "gut" to tell us the right thing to do.

The "grotto" – getting away from it all,
just a few steps from our back door.

Choose your most empowering tips from the ones suggested below and use them to take the right action for you.

Tips for Overcoming Your Fears About Cooperative Householding

Fact Seeking — Use facts to confront fear.	Problem-Solving — Dissolve your fear step by step.
• Read articles and books about what it is like to live in a cooperative household. • Attend a conference about cooperative householding to learn how others dealt with their fears. • Talk with a financial advisor or realtors about options. • Check your interpretations and conclusions with others.	• Find an action-oriented, self-help book on overcoming fears. Set aside an hour a day to follow the steps. • Create a plan. And create a Plan B in case your first plan falls through.
Social Connection — Give away your fear to the group.	**Intuition — Transform your fear into an animal of power.**
• Participate in local groups or online discussion groups with people who have done something similar. • Make a commitment to yourself by making a commitment to others – tell your friends and family what you are going to do. • Avoid naysayers and find people who can help you think things through realistically.	• Draw a picture of where you are now and where you want to be. Now draw the events that will occur along the way. • Use spiritual practices like meditation, yoga, or going for a walk. • Write about what you have accomplished in a journal. • Imagine yourself living happily in a cooperative household. How did you make that happen?

What Does Your Gut Say?

We have given you lots to think about and, we hope, some exercises to prepare you for creating your own cooperative household. But ultimately, as Jean points out, the final decision is intuitive. At some point, your "gut" tells you that this is for you. That is the point at which you should march forward with confidence to form your own version of a cooperative household.

Life is good.

Hearth and home.

Epilogue

Aparticularly thoughtful workshop participant once asked us two questions that stumped us: *"How have you changed as a result of this experience? What have you learned about yourselves through this experience?"*

Certainly we have changed, and we think we've changed for the better. In these reflections, now many years into our cooperative household, we seek to answer those questions. We hope that our "up close and personal" reflections will be useful to you.

Jean:

It is surreal to think that we have been living in this lovely old house for these many years. It was such a leap of faith when we moved here...three strong women, so completely different from one another...sometimes I wonder what made us so sure it would work. I knew it would though, on a deep level, and I believe that Karen and Louise knew, too. On the surface it seemed outside the box, but we knew it was a small risk we were taking.

And we have been proven right. What a great choice we made in making this 70-year-old colonial our home. We have made it our own: wallpaper and paint in most rooms to update the look; hardwood floors refinished in a rich cherry; new and simpler window treatments to bring in the light. Almost all the gardens surrounding the house and backyard have been reworked and renewed. We all take such pleasure in caring for and maintaining our home.

My personal journey has been enriched by the experience of living here at Shadowlawn. I am proud of this lovely, funky, eclectic place, and I am comforted by the ambiance we have created. I love sitting by the living room fire in the winter, working or reading or just chatting with my "communards." In winter we can be found down in the "rumpus room" watching movies. (Louise and I make it our mission to see all films nominated for Academy Awards before the ceremony – and Karen indulges us by joining when she can.)

In summertime the backyard, surrounded by gardens and mature trees, is like a cathedral where we find respite from the frenetic pace of our work lives. A familiar summer scene is Louise on a chaise in the backyard with an open book, napping.

Late nights often find us sitting at a table in the far reaches of the backyard, "the grotto," enjoying a glass of wine. For some of our friends, a late night trip to the grotto is an anticipated treat.

The side porch is another outdoor refuge, where the spectacular climbing hydrangea embraces the space and creates a peaceful resting place (when the ubiquitous neighborhood power tools are finally quiet and the tinkling wind chimes can be heard). Summer meals on the side porch are particularly wonderful.

I especially enjoy those times when all three of us find ourselves in the same room, each with her laptop, e-mailing articles or ideas to the others. Often, we are in the garden room in summer or winter, as it looks out over the backyard surrounded by tall trees, lovely in any season.

Year 'round, there are birds at the feeders. Goldfinches, house finches, wrens and chickadees stop by for a treat, along with blue jays, cardinals and an occasional downy woodpecker. The juncos and mourning doves share the seeds on the ground with the squirrels. One year, the lighted deer lawn ornament named Harry David appeared in the backyard at Christmastime.

My third-floor suite is another favorite refuge. I love my perch at the top of the house, a private space where I can work in my office or relax or read in my bedroom. Our private spaces are part of the magic here – we knew that our house needed to provide us with the right mix of private and shared space.

A real surprise was realizing that if one is going to be at the house on Halloween after dark, one must be prepared to turn off the lights and watch some of the scariest, most nerve-wracking movies ever made, while waiting for the sweet costumed children to ring the doorbell. Although this contrast may seem incongruous, Louise considers this the appropriate genre for the occasion and we have not ever been able to skip this aspect of observing the day. To be honest, I have come to rather look forward to Halloween, sweet children and scary movies.

The relationships we have built with each other are a very important aspect of what works at Shadowlawn. Each of us has strengths and skills to share, and we offer them freely. Chores are shared with no need to write up a schedule. We are good friends and we have become sisters of the heart, completely trusting one another and accepting one another as we are, imperfect as that may be.

We don't always agree, and sometimes one or more of us

may not be completely happy with a joint decision, but we always knew there would be compromise in a communal living arrangement. And virtually all of those joint decisions turned out just fine.

My greatest concern was being able to assert myself with these two very powerful women – in my marriage I had learned this skill (perhaps this is why I ultimately divorced), but that didn't seem to guarantee that I would be successful in a group of three. I generally can compromise and there could be no doubt that a cooperative household is all about compromise. However, there are times when one has to speak up and let her voice be heard and I have found that I am well able to do that when I have strong feelings.

Remember the example – the night when, preparing for our first Christmas in the house, Louise and Karen went to buy more tree lights and came back with the old-fashioned large bulbs that I do not like. I hadn't been consulted and I made my feelings heard. When people ask us if we've ever had a "fight," this experience with the Christmas lights is what first comes to mind.

After all the planning we did for this venture, even after jointly writing a Partnership Agreement, this was the first time we were quite consciously aware of the delicate balance that needs to be kept when collaborating on even seemingly minor decisions. This confirmed that I could hold my own; guess I didn't really need to worry about that.

I am happy that each of us agrees that a house is not a home without a cat. Beardsley was the original cat-alyst who started this adventure into shared living; she could never be replaced, but she passed on her legacy to Kali (see below).

Shadowlawn has become my home, as well as my house. It is sometimes quite seductive; I often find it very easy to deny the reality of having to create my means of retirement. Our time here will be limited by our ability to manage it physically, mentally, and financially. It is interesting to consider that we originally talked about retiring together, but now the conversation is of communal living now, and retiring separately.

This is the right place to be right now. The future will unfold as it will, though I will do what I can to create and design it to my specifications. I can't imagine not living in a shared living situation, especially as I get older.

Karen:

Our living arrangement has been more than I hoped. True to expectation, we realized all of the convenience and financial benefits we planned for. Our estimate of monthly costs proved more than reasonable; we have had to increase our contribution only once, by $100 per month. With our budgeting, we have not only maintained but have improved our house and property. When the day finally comes to sell this place, we should find we have made a much better investment than our previous living arrangements, despite the difficult economic times.

The surprise to me is how our relationships have evolved. I'm sure you felt the tenuous tone of our first year. We all knew this would work; we all bent over backwards to make it work, but without giving up our own sense of self, without sacrificing our own needs, be they for privacy or family.

We have become more than friends – close to being family without the obligations. Rather like three sisters who get along, enjoy one another's company, yet go their own ways.

Our family circles feel larger now. Some of Jean's relatives have celebrated weddings here. Louise's family has moved their Christmas from the traditional family home to our place. My family (nine of them) has stayed here all at once to celebrate our own Christmas. We have a wonderful sense of friendship and extended family, sometimes mixing all the groups.

I've learned much from my two housemates. I've learned how to better fulfill my own value of helping other people. I've learned that it's okay not to be perfect, nor do things perfectly. On the lighter side, I've learned a bunch of tips for making life easier and conserving resources. One does not need to wash a blouse every time she wears it! It's okay to use partially burned candles when guests come from dinner. And the rugs don't need to be sent for cleaning every year.

On more serious matters, I've learned to be more attentive to and respectful of the views of other people. My family jokes that we grew up in a house where we learned we always were right – to the extreme! When I was a young teenager, my mother died and my father subsequently remarried. I "welcomed" my new step-mother by explaining to her how to properly fold the towels and put them in the linen closet. I think about that absurd rigidity every time I look at our common linen closet or at the messy heap of towels in my own bathroom. Life is better when one is less dogmatic, more flexible. Conversations are easier; friendships are deeper. Living in a cooperative household has greatly enhanced that learning about myself.

Annoyances? Not really. If anything, I get annoyed when we duplicate food we already have, or when a "helping" housemate interferes with something I'm doing – like someone closing the garage door when I've purposely left it up. But those are momentary annoyances of little import. Besides, I too duplicate food and help too much.

But I am not one for looking back. I look forward. Way forward. After all, I'm the one who started all of this by talking about a long-term plan for retirement. During the past few years, I have once again looked forward. And taken action. In keeping with my preference for a warmer climate, I've chosen my retirement spot – far away from Pittsburgh. That decision rocked the boat a bit at Shadowlawn, possibly because Jean and Louise were concerned about how soon the shift would occur.

The residence I chose for retirement is quite different from Shadowlawn. The choice of a condo is obvious for someone who will be approaching 70. Condos minimize the upkeep that will become progressively more challenging as I age. But many other factors went into the choice.

First of all, I chose a place with three bedrooms and two baths in a split design. The master bedroom and bath are at one end; the other two bedrooms and bath are at the other end. In between are lanai, living room, dining room, kitchen and a hallway. Both bedroom areas are as private as one can get in a condo. You've probably guessed my plan. My hope is that this spot, too, will be a shared housing arrangement. The benefits of Shadowlawn are too good to give up! The best of all worlds would be for Jean, Louise or both of them to join me for this next step in life.

Prior to selecting my location, I was fortunate to learn of Louis Tenenbaum's work on Aging in Place. Tenenbaum is dedicated to a movement that will provide the infrastructure for individuals to remain in their environment of choice much longer and to stay healthier and happier than our current systems support. In his "MetLife Report on Aging in Place 2.0," he sees two categories of infrastructure needed to support long-term, independent living.

1. *Connections to the world outside the home: technology, community resources, and transportation and community infrastructure*

2. *Home design, devices and assistive technologies to reduce risk and facilitate wise and effective use of resources*

I can't single-handedly create transportation systems or community infrastructures. But I can and did select a location that optimizes my use of existing systems. My new place is walking distance from many activities I enjoy and is on a bus line that will take me anywhere I need to go. I also deliberately chose a place that requires renovation. That means I got it for a very reasonable price and can afford to design it for my specifications. When I renovate it, I will pay close attention to the advice from Aging in Place experts regarding supporting technology. For one, I'll install bathroom amenities that make life easier and safer for older people.

So when will I retire? When will I move away from Shadow-lawn, from this community? I will move when Jean and Louise are ready to take their next steps in life, as well. I believe in what we are doing; I love our relationships and our home; I won't be the one to break it up. May I be so fortunate to have one or both of them join me in the next step of life.

Louise:

For me, the biggest surprise about cooperative householding is how much easier it is than I had expected. In any living situation – family, spouse, friends – there are tradeoffs, pros and cons. But, nine years in, the benefits of cohouseholding vastly overshadow the tradeoffs.

Bottom line: I love where, how, and with whom I'm living. In this special house, the spirit of shared adventure makes every day feel new and fresh.

How much relates to the individual personalities versus the cohouseholding model? Who knows? I do know that life is richer and my experiences have been broadened. Because our work is shared, there are more flowers in the garden, better and more varied food, and many more social connections and events at the house than I would ever attempt alone. There is also warmth, love and laughter.

My brother, Art, wonders if our success is enhanced by the generous physical space of this house, and the commonalities in our professional training and backgrounds. I agree: that's part of the equation. We were able to choose a house with lots of space – indeed, virtual suites – and our training in psychology, healthcare and behavioral science helps us recognize and deal with the dynamics of interpersonal relationships.

But other factors have been just as important. We all get a huge energy charge out of being independent together, taking care of business in smart ways, learning and doing. Mundane tasks have felt like adventures. At first daunted, I've grown to enjoy changing the old-fashioned gaslight mantles, balancing on a high stepladder and clinging to the lamp pole. Here's the important part: Jean and Karen are always there, supporting the ladder. Didn't think I could do it the first time, but now it's a piece of cake.

One of our home maintenance projects literally put a bug in my ear. A tiny ant crawled in while I was removing a shutter from the ivy-covered brick wall. For a week, I thought it was water bubbling around in my head until the ant crawled out. Yuck! Moral of the story: live and learn. Try new things. Stretch. Suck it up when yucky things happen, but enjoy telling the story later.

At Shadowlawn, I've learned to work extra hard at self-control. Unlike the expectations within a family, we knew from the start that this partnership would not be permanent. I for one don't take anything or anyone for granted. This situation is too good to risk messing up.

I am continually amazed at how multi-faceted and complex people are; when you live with other people, you are reminded on a daily basis. My responsible, smart and well-organized partners have their inconsistencies and foibles; I do, too.

People ask if there is a downside to cohouseholding. I answer, "Not really." Some annoying stuff happens in any household where people live together, as it also did when I lived alone. The biggest disappointments: occasional minor oversights that cause waste or inefficiency or security problems: the refrigerator door left open, the stove burner left on, the side door ajar, candles burning down, and – icing on the cake – the garden hose left dripping for three months, leaking into the basement. I have likely been the unwitting culprit at times, although it is human nature to hope it was someone else's error. I've learned it's best not to blame.

However, those occasional lapses have an impact. I fight the impulse to over-compensate or control by increasing my vigilance. While I rarely worry about anything, I tend to think proactively and notice details. I try to be subtle when I double-check to be sure lights are out, doors are locked; usually they are, but sometimes they're not. In a traditional family setting, I might yell at the suspected culprit; here, I don't.

I thought long and hard about that provocative question, *How have you changed?* I kept coming up blank. Am I less controlling? Am I more flexible? Neater? Better able to compromise? Any better able to be a team player? Hmm...better ask the housemates what they think. But suddenly I knew my answer. *I am happier.*

So – ask me about the Shadowlawn adventure and I'll speak in fluent cliché, but it's just the plain truth. We've all expanded our horizons and our capabilities. We've lived far better for far less. All for one and one for all. Wouldn't change a thing. No regrets. Life is good.

Beardsley: R.I.P.

The Last B-Mail

From: lmachinist
Date: April 20 10:30:55 PM EST
To: Karen Bush
Subject: B-mail

Dear Karen,

Did Big One and Quick One tell you how good I have been at night? I've been sleeping like a log, 'cause my tummy has been full. The kibble is extra yummy and smells so meaty with hot water mixed in. I guess I'm getting too old to chomp hard kibble, so sometimes I don't even bother.

It's been the cat's meow, living here with three humans to spoil me and four toilets to drink out of.

Love,
Beardsley

P.S. No matter what happens, I know that you will never find another cat as wonderful as me.

Sadly, we lost Beardsley when she reached the ripe old age of 19. We'd like to think that her years with all of us at Shadowlawn were her best. In her honor, we continue to call our annual trips "The Annual Beardsley Guilt Trips."

Introducing Kali:

For a black cat, I sure am lucky. I was a tiny stray, rescued by some nice old folks. They couldn't keep me because I "ran them ragged." Then one day, three strange humans came to visit. I entertained them by climbing, knocking things over, hiding behind the furniture. It worked. I got a new home where I am the Alpha Cat.

They named me for Kali, the Hindu goddess of destruction, but I just like to play...glassware and toilet paper are my specialties.

Beardsley – I try to continue your legacy by chasing the chipmunks. I heard that you liked to eat them, but I prefer to beg in the kitchen for kibble.

Kali

Kali strikes again!

General Partnership
Agreement

Below is the General Partnership Agreement that we developed with professional legal advice for our cooperative household in Pittsburgh, Pennsylvania. We offer it as an example, not a recommendation.

Anyone entering into a cooperative household arrangement should work with an attorney to develop legal documents appropriate to their situation, municipality and state.

The Agreement

D. Jean McQuillin of (County), (State); Louise S. Machinist of (County), (State); and Karen M. Bush, of (County), (State), (the "Partners") agree as follows:

Type of Partnership. The parties voluntarily associate themselves together as general partners for the purpose of conducting the general business of acquiring, owning, developing, mortgaging, encumbering, maintaining, improving, altering, remodeling, expanding, and otherwise operating and dealing with the real property located at (Address) (the "Property") including, without limitation, obtaining financing and refinancing for the above purposes, and any other businesses that may from time to time be agreed on by the Partners.

Name of Partnership. The name of the Partnership shall be *Shadowlawn* Cooperative.

Term of Partnership. This Partnership shall commence on (Date) and shall continue until dissolved by mutual agreement of the parties or terminated as provided in this Agreement.

Capital Commitment. The capital commitment of this Partnership shall be the sum of $_____, to which each Partner shall contribute $_____ by depositing that amount in a checking account in the name of the Partnership or by purchasing or procuring an insurance policy with a death benefit in that amount, naming the remaining partners as the beneficiaries, on or before (Date).

Additional Contributions. The Partners must contribute equally, on a monthly basis, to cover the costs of debt and utility service and general maintenance of the Property.

Withdrawal of Capital. No Partner shall withdraw any portion of the capital of the Partnership without the express written consent of the other Partners.

Assets and Debts. Any net assets or debts that may accrue to the Partnership shall be distributed to or borne by the Partners in equal proportions.

Partnership Books. At all times during the continuation of the Partnership, the Partners shall keep accurate books of account in which all matters relating to the Partnership, including all of its income, expenditures, assets, and liabilities, shall be entered. These books shall be kept on a cash basis and shall be open to examination by any Partner at any time.

Title to Partnership Property. All real or personal property acquired by the Partnership, including all improvements placed or located on that property, shall be owned by and in the name of the Partnership, that ownership being subject to the other terms and provisions of this Agreement. Each Partner expressly waives the right to require partition of any Partnership Property or any part of it. The Partners shall execute any documents that may be necessary to reflect the Partnership's ownership of its assets and shall record the same in the public offices that may be necessary or desirable in the discretion of the Partners.

Fiscal Year. The fiscal year of the Partnership shall end on the 31st day of December each year.

Authority. Each Partner shall have equal authority to bind the Partnership in making contracts and incurring obligations in the name and on the credit of the Partnership solely for emergencies related to the house or land. No Partner shall incur any obligations in the name or on the credit of the Partnership exceeding $2500 without the express written consent of the other Partners. Any obligation incurred in violation of this provision shall be charged to and collected from the individual Partner incurring the obligation.

Unauthorized occupancy. No parties other than the three Partners may reside at the property for more than seven (7) consecutive days or twenty-one (21) total days per year without written authorization by all three Partners.

Net Profits Defined. The term "net profits" as used in this Agreement shall mean the net profits of the Partnership as determined by generally accepted accounting principles for each accounting period provided for in this Agreement.

Assignment or Transfer of Partnership Interest. No Partner may assign or transfer her interest in the Partnership. With written consent of the remaining Partners, a Partner may sublease her space. Subleasing does not imply any rights of Partnership.

Voluntary Withdrawal of Partner. Any Partner may withdraw for any reason by giving the other Partners not less than two months written notice of her intention to do so.

Involuntary Withdrawal of Partner. Any Partner who is unable, for any reason, to fulfill her monthly payment obligations to the Partnership for two (2) consecutive months shall, upon the passing of the second month, be notified by the Partnership that she must withdraw from the Partnership no later than two (2) months from the date of that notice. The withdrawing Partner must comply with that notice by withdrawing within the two (2) month period.

Structural Changes. Modifications to the structure require agreement of all three Partners. A Partner may complete an agreed upon modification at her expense; however, said Partner assumes full responsibility and liability for ensuring proper construction techniques and meeting of all structural codes.

Irresolvable Differences. If any irresolvable difference arises among the three Partners, any Partner may initiate mediation with a professional mediator, with a duration no longer than three (3) hours. Should mediation fail to resolve the differences, the partners will submit the dispute to binding arbitration by a professional arbitrator and will comply with the decision of the arbitrator, including involuntary withdrawal from the Partnership. All expenses incurred for mediation and arbitration are to be paid by the partnership.

Buyout of Terminated Interest. If the Partnership is dissolved by the withdrawal of a Partner from this Agreement, the withdrawing Partner shall be required to sell her interest in the Partnership to the Partnership for an amount equal to one-third (1/3) of the value of the property, less any encumbrances. This value is to be determined within 15 business days of notice of termination, evaluated by a professional, residential real estate appraiser, as of the date that written notice of withdrawal is tendered to the Partnership (in the case of voluntary withdrawal) or to the withdrawing Partner (in the case of involuntary withdrawal). Payment of this amount shall be made to the withdrawing partner in twelve (12) equal monthly installments commencing the date of the acceptance of the appraisal. After payment of such consideration, the withdrawing Partner shall thereafter have no interest of any kind whatsoever in the Partnership, its assets, or business.

Buy-Sell on Death of Partner. If the Partnership is dissolved by the death of a Partner, the remaining Partners shall have the obligation to purchase the interest of the deceased Partner in the Partnership and to pay to the personal representative of the deceased Partner the value of that interest as provided in Paragraph 19 of this Agreement. The remaining Partners may continue the business of the Partnership but the estate or personal representative of the deceased Partner shall not be liable for any obligations incurred in the Partnership business subsequent to the Partner's death. The estate of the deceased Partner shall be obligated to sell her Partnership interest as provided in this Agreement.

Duties of Purchasing Partners. On any purchase and sale pursuant to the provisions of Paragraph 19 or 20 of this Agreement, the remaining Partners shall assume all obligations of the Partnership and shall hold the withdrawing Partner, the personal representative and estate of a deceased Partner, and the property of any withdrawing or deceased Partner free and harmless from all liability for these obligations. Furthermore, the remaining Partners, at their own expense, shall immediately cause to be prepared, filed, served, and published all notices that may be required by law to protect the withdrawing Partner or the personal representative or estate of a deceased Partner from liability for the future obligations of the Partnership business.

Notices. All notices between the parties provided for or permitted under this Agreement or by law shall be in writing and shall be deemed duly served when personally delivered to a Partner or, instead of personal service, when deposited in the United States mail, as certified, with postage prepaid, and addressed to the Partner at the address of the principal place of business of the Partnership.

Consents and Agreements. All consents and agreements provided for or permitted by this Agreement shall be in writing and a signed copy of them shall be filed and kept with the records of the Partnership.

Entire Agreement. This instrument contains the entire agreement of the parties relating to their Partnership and correctly sets forth the rights, duties, and obligations of each to the others in connection with it as of its date. Any prior agreements, promises, negotiations, or representations not expressly set forth in this Agreement are of no force or effect.

The signatures below indicate a good faith promise to abide by the conditions stated in this DRAFT document.

If I try hard enough, I can push it over...

Resources

Organizations

Aging In Community. www.agingincommunity.com

Baby Boomer Lifeboat: Affordable baby boomers retirement housing. www.babyboomerlifeboat.com/baby_boomer_low_cost_housing.htm

CoAbode: Single Mothers Homesharing. www.coabode.org

The Cohousing Association of the United States, www.cohousing.org

Women Living in Community, www.womenlivingincommunity.com

The Transition Network, www.thetransitionnetwork.org

The Fellowship for Intentional Community, http://fic.ic.org

The Federation of Egalitarian Communities, http://thefec.org

The Senior Cooperative Foundation, www.seniorcoops.org

Senior Home Sharing, Inc., www.seniorhomesharing.org

Publications

Barrette, E. "Householding: Communal Living on a Small Scale." *Communities Magazine*. Fall 2009 issue, #144.

Bennett, A. *The Uncommon Reader.* London: Faber and Faber, Inc., 2006.

Chapin, R. *Pocket Neighborhoods: Creating Small-Scale Community in a Large-Scale World.* Newtown, Conn: Taunton, 2011.

Chiras, D., Wann, D. *Superbia: 31 Ways to Create Sustainable Neighborhoods.* Gabriola Island, B.C., Canada: New Society, 2003.

Christian, D. L. *Finding Community: How to Join an Ecovillage or Intentional Community.* Gabriola Island, B.C., Canada: New Society, 2007.

Communities Directory: A Comprehensive Guide to Intentional Communities and Cooperative Living. Fellowship for Intentional Community, 2010.

Communities Magazine. Fellowship for Intentional Community. Print and online versions. http://communities.ic.org

Dawson, J. *Ecovillages: New Frontiers for Sustainability, Schumacher Briefing No. 12* (Schumacher Briefings). Devon, United Kingdom: Green Books, 2006.

Doskow, E., Orsi, J. *The Sharing Solution: How to Save Money, Simplify Your Life & Build Community.* Berkeley, Calif.: Nolo, 2009.

Durrett, C. *The Senior Cohousing Handbook: A Community Approach to Independent Living.* Gabriola Island, BC, Canada: New Society, 2009.

Durrett, C., McCamant, K. *Creating Cohousing: Building Sustainable Communities.* Gabriola Island, B.C., Canada: New Society, 2011.

Klinenberg, E. *Going Solo: The Extraordinary Rise and Surprising Appeal of Living Alone.* Penguin, 2012.

Kushner, H. S. *When Bad Things Happen to Good People.* New York: Random House, 1981.

Litchfield, M. *In-laws, Outlaws, and Granny Flats: Your Guide to Turning One House into Two Homes.* Newtown, Conn.: Taunton, 2011.

Marohn, S. *Audacious Aging: Eldership as a Revolutionary Endeavor.* Fulton, Calif.: Elite Books, 2009.

McCamant, K. M, Durrett, C., Hertzman, E., Moore, C. W. *Cohousing: A Contemporary Approach to Housing Ourselves.* Berkeley, Calif.: Ten Speed Press, 1994.

Medlicott, J. *The Ladies of Covington Send Their Love.* New York: Thomas Dunne, 2000.

Meltzer, G., Ph.D. *Sustainable Community: Learning from the Cohousing Model.* Bloomington, Ind.: Trafford, 2005.

Miller, M. *The Hard Times Guide to Retirement Security: Practical Strategies for Money, Work, and Living.* Hoboken, N.J.: Bloomberg Press (Wiley), 2010. http://retirementrevised.com

Mollison, B. *Introduction to Permaculture.* Tasmania, Australia: Tagari, 1997.

Pitkin, J., Myers, D. "Driving and the Built Environment: The Effects of Compact Development on Motorized Travel, Energy Use, and CO_2 Emissions." Committee for the Study on the Relationships Among Development Patterns, Vehicle Miles Traveled, and Energy Consumption. Transportation Research Board Special Report 298. National Research Council of the National Academies. 2009.

Porcino, J. *Living Longer, Living Better: Adventures in Community Housing for Those in the Second Half of Life.* New York: Continuum International Publishing Group, 1991.

Puhar, A. *Sharing Housing: A Guidebook to Finding and Keeping Good Housemates.* Peterborough, N.H.: Bauhan, 2011.

Ray, P. Ph.D., Anderson, S. R. *The Cultural Creatives: How 50 Million People Are Changing the World.* New York: Three Rivers, 2001.

Reed, J., Chendea, J., Costa, J. *Co-op Villages.* Pensacola, Fla. Co-Op Village Foundation, Inc., 2007.

Reza, Y. *Art.* New York: Faber and Faber, Inc., 1997.

Rosenfeld, J. P., Chapman, W. *Unassisted Living.* New York: Monacelli Press, 2011.

ScottHanson, C., ScottHanson, K. *The Cohousing Handbook: Building a Place for Community.* Gabriola Island, B.C., Canada: New Society, 2004.

Shaffer, C. R. *Creating Community Anywhere.* United Kingdom: CCC Press, 2005

Stephens, L. *House Mates: A Guide to Cooperative Shared Housing.* Portland, Ore.: Verbatim, 1997.

Tenenbaum, L. "The MetLife Report on Aging in Place 2.0: Rethinking Solutions to the Home Care Challenge." September 2010. (Available online as a pdf)

Online

"Being Alone Together." *New York Times.* 12 February 2012. www.nytimes.com/roomfordebate/2012/02/12/the-advantages-and-disadvantages-of-living-alone/living-single-happily-and-differently

Brandt, E. Ph.D. "Back To Sophisticated Communes – Will Baby Boomers Come Full Circle? Scott's Story." 18 August 2009. http://angriestgeneration.wordpress.com/2009/08/18/back-to-sophisticated-communes-will-baby-boomers-come-full-circle-scotts-story

Cappello, R. "For Boomers, a Thousand Flavors of Retirement." Huffington Post. 19 September 2012. www.huffingtonpost.com/ron-cappello/retirement_b_1894904.html

Eberlein, S. "Life Is Easier With Friends Next Door: Feeling a need for community? Cohousing can provide affordable space and neighbors to share it with." *Yes!* magazine. 16 July 2012. www.yesmagazine.org/issues/making-it-home/life-is-easier-with-friends-next-door

Green, P. "Under One Roof: Building for Extended Families." *New York Times.* 30 November 2012. www.nytimes.com/2012/11/30/us/building-homes-for-modern-multigenerational-families.html?emc=eta1

"Housing Vacancies and Homeownership." U.S. Gov. www.census.gov/housing/hvs

Levine, R. "My House Our House." *mt. lebanon magazine.* July 2012. http://lebomag.com/5213/my-house-our-house

Mann, T. "Mature Market Experts' Gem of the Day: Shared Housing – The Next Senior Trend?" Mature Market Experts. December 2012. http://trmann.com/wordpress/2010/12/mature-market-experts%E2%80%99-gem-of-the-day-shared-housing-the-next-senior-trend

Ray, P.H. Ph.D. "Cultural Creatives and the Emerging Planetary Wisdom Culture." http://culturalcreatives.org/who-we-are/

Russ, M. "House Sharing Becomes More Common With Down Economy." KPBS. 18 March 2009. www.kpbs.org/news/2009/mar/18/house-sharing-becomes-more-common-with-down/

Stinson, S. "How to Live Cheaply in Retirement With Roommates." Fox Business News. 21 August 2012. www.foxbusiness.com/personal-finance/2012/08/21/how-to-live-cheaply-in-retirement-with-roommates

Spinner, A. "Peace, Love, and Social Security: Baby Boomers Retire to the Commune." *The Atlantic.* 21 November 2011. www.theatlantic.com/national/archive/2011/11/peace-love-and-social-security-baby-boomers-retire-to-the-commune/248583

Winter, A. "House Sharing Trend Grows Among Seniors." National Aging in Place Council. 12 June 2011. www2.tbo.com/shopping/homeseeker/2011/jun/12/house-sharing-trend-grows-among-seniors-ar-235956

Acknowledgments

It takes a community...
Our cooperative household has been enriched by many warm and wonderful relationships. We send our love and thanks to the mentors, friends, and family members (overlapping categories) who urged us to write this book and supported our long on-and-off writing odyssey.

Thank you, relatives, for your written reflections and/or wise advice: Maureen Bailey, Goldyn Daupin, Karen's nieces Tania and Dana, Art and Ed Steinmark. To the friends who, way back at the beginning, critiqued our first draft: we haven't forgotten! We treasure your gifts of time and honest feedback.

Thank you, Fred Schroyer, our fabulous first first-edition editor, Karen's long-time colleague and friend. When asked if we should abandon MHOH after our initial tentative draft, Fred's response sustained us: *It's a good story. You should publish it.* His gentle nudging over the years *(Where's your book?)* spurred us to completion.

Thank you, John Armstrong, our fabulous, eagle-eyed *second* first-edition editor, proofreader, wordsmith, mentor and friend. Rutabaga casserole any time you want it!

Much appreciation to Ruth Rocap, librarian, Louise's high school buddy, for gifting us our first Library of Congress number; and to "KZ" Zoller: warm memories of the book launch party still touch our hearts.

We are ever-grateful to reporters Rita Levine, *mt. lebanon magazine*, and Virginia Linn, *Pittsburgh Post-Gazette*, for telling our story and thus inadvertently introducing us to Paul Kelly, publisher of St. Lynn's Press. Dear Paul: thank you for seeing the value in our work and reaching out.

To the St Lynn's Press team, Cathy Dees, editor; Holly Rosborough, book designer and photographer; and Marguerite Nocchi, editorial intern: We loved working with you! Thank you for your elegant transformation of *My House Our House*.

We are indebted to Louis Tenenbaum for the gift of a big-picture-perspective book foreword, and for giving us a deeper understanding of Aging in Place; and to Sally Abrahms for introducing us to Louis.

Thank you, Oz Ragland, former Executive Director of the Cohousing Association of the United States and The Cohouse-holding Project instigator/investigator, who welcomed us newcomers into the wider network of intentional community. We are energized as we connect to living-in-community colleagues, in particular Marianne Kilkenny, Maria Piantanida, Annamarie Pluhar, and Linda Williams.

And finally, a posthumous virtual chin scratch and kibble treat to Beardsley, for bringing us together.

About the Authors

Karen M. Bush, Ph.D.: Consultant, teacher, mentor, writer, traveler, tinkerer and photographer. Karen's fondest hope is that My House Our House inspires the thousands of people who live alone to take the leap to the joy of living in community.

Louise S. Machinist, M.A.: Licensed Clinical Psychologist, reader, singer, and intellectually curious individual. Louise is proud to be part of the "Innovative Generation." The gathering wave of lifestyle change is here! She hopes people will benefit from the catalyst of our experience and how-to ideas.

Jean McQuillin, B.S., R.N.: Professional nurse, business owner, mentor, coach, mom, grandma, independent woman and lover of people and life. Jean's mission is to help others get from where they are to where they want to be – knowing that the only real risk is not to take one. The first step for many may be picking up *My House Our House!*

Karen, Louise and Jean are honored to be on the Advisory Board for The Cohouseholding Project/Cohouseholding.com.

Our book is our bio. Take a walk through our virtual door to get to know us better.

www.myhouseourhouse.com

on Facebook: www.facebook.com/MyHouseOurHouse

on Twitter @myhouseourhouse

Our house is a very, very, very fine house...